An Introduction to English Morphology

Words and Their Structure

Andrew Carstairs-McCarthy

Edinburgh University Press

To Jeremy

© Andrew Carstairs-McCarthy, 2002

Edinburgh University Press Ltd
22 George Square, Edinburgh

Reprinted 2004, 2005

Typeset in Janson
by Norman Tilley Graphics and
printed and bound in Great Britain
by MPG Books Ltd, Bodmin

A CIP Record for this book is available from the British Library

ISBN 0 7486 1327 7 (hardback)
ISBN 0 7486 1326 9 (paperback)

The right of Andrew Carstairs-McCarthy
to be identified as author of this work
has been asserted in accordance with
the Copyright, Designs and Patents Act 1988.

Contents

Acknowledgements

I would like to thank Heinz Giegerich for inviting me to write this book, and him and Laurie Bauer for useful comments on a draft version. I must admit that, when I set out to write what is intended as an introductory text on an extremely well-described language, I did not expect to learn anything new myself; but I have enjoyed discovering and rediscovering both new and old questions that arise from the study of morphology and its interaction with syntax and the lexicon, even if I cannot claim to have provided any conclusive new answers.

The Library of the University of Canterbury has, as always, been efficient in supplying research material. I would also like to thank my partner Jeremy Carstairs-McCarthy for constant support and help.

1 Introduction

The term 'word' is part of everyone's vocabulary. We all think we understand what words are. What's more, we are right to think this, at some level. In this book I will not suggest that our ordinary notion of the word needs to be replaced with something radically different. Rather, I want to show how our ordinary notion can be made more precise. This will involve teasing apart the bundle of ingredients that go to make up the notion, showing how these ingredients interact, and introducing ways of talking about each one separately. After reading this book, you will still go on using the term 'word' in talking about language, both in everyday conversation and in more formal contexts, such as literary criticism or English language study; but I hope that, in these more formal contexts, you will talk about words more confidently, knowing exactly which ingredients of the notion you have in mind at any one time, and able where necessary to use appropriate terminology in order to make your meaning absolutely clear.

This is a textbook for students of the English language or of English literature, not primarily for students of linguistics. Nevertheless, what I say will be consistent with mainstream linguistic views on word-structure, so any readers who go on to more advanced linguistics will not encounter too many inconsistencies.

A good way of teasing apart the ingredients in the notion 'word' is by explicitly contrasting them. Here are the contrasts that we will be looking at, and the chapters where they will be discussed:

- words as *units of meaning* versus *units of sentence structure* (Chapters 2, 6, 7)
- words as *pronounceable* entities ('word forms') versus *more abstract* entities (sets of word forms) (Chapters 3, 4, 5)
- *inflectionally related* word forms (forms of *the same* 'word') versus *derivationally related* words (*different* 'words' with a shared base) (Chapters 4, 5)

1

- the distinction between *compound words* and *phrases* (Chapters 6, 7)
- the relationship between the *internal structure* of a word and its *meaning* (Chapter 7)
- *productive* versus *unproductive* word-forming processes (Chapter 8)
- historical reasons for some of the contemporary divisions within English morphology, especially *Germanic* versus *Romance* word-formation processes (Chapter 9).

These various contrasts impact on one another in various ways. For example, if one takes the view that the distinction between compound words and phrases is unimportant, or is even perhaps a bogus distinction fundamentally, this will have a considerable effect on how one views the word as a unit of sentence-structure. Linguistic scholars who specialise in the study of words (so-called 'morphologists') devote considerable effort to working out the implications of different ways of formulating these distinctions, as they strive to discover the best way (that is, the most illuminating way, or the way that seems to accord most accurately with people's implicit knowledge of their native languages). We will not be exploring the technical ramifications of these efforts in this book. Nevertheless, I will need to ensure that the way I draw the distinctions here yields a coherent overall picture, and some cross-referencing between chapters will be necessary for that.

Each of Chapters 2 to 9 inclusive is provided with exercises. This is designed to make the book suitable for a course extending over about ten weeks. Relatively full discussions of the exercises are also provided at the end of the book. For those exercises that are open-ended (that is, ones for which there is no obvious 'right' answer), these discussions serve to illustrate and extend points made in the chapter.

As befits a book aimed at students of English rather than linguistics students, references to the technical literature are kept to a minimum. However, the 'Recommendations for reading' at the end of each chapter contain some hints for any readers who would like to delve into this literature, as well as pointing towards more detailed treatments of English morphology in particular.

Finally, I would like to encourage comments and criticisms. My choice of what to emphasise and what to leave out will inevitably not please everyone, nor will some of the details of what I say. I hope, however, that even those who find things to disagree with in this book will also find it useful for its intended introductory purpose, whether as students, teachers or general readers.

Recommendations for reading

At the end of each chapter are recommendations for reading relating to the subject-matter of the chapter. Here I offer some comments on general works dealing with English or morphology or both.

Of the available books on English morphology in particular, Bauer (1983) delves deepest into issues of linguistic theory (although a now somewhat dated version of it), and offers useful discussion and case-studies of fashions in derivational morphology. Marchand (1969) is factually encyclopedic. Adams (1973) concentrates on compounding (the subject-matter of our Chapter 6) and conversion (discussed here in Chapter 5), but says relatively little about derivation (covered here in Chapter 5).

There is no book that deals adequately with morphology in general linguistic terms and that also takes into account fully up-to-date versions of syntactic and phonological theory. Bauer (1988) is a clear introductory text. The main strength of Matthews (1991) is its terminological precision. Carstairs-McCarthy (1992) is aimed at readers whose knowledge of linguistics is at advanced undergraduate level or beyond. Spencer (1991) covers much ground, and may be said to bridge the gap between Bauer and Carstairs-McCarthy.

2 Words, sentences and dictionaries

2.1 Words as meaningful building-blocks of language

We think of words as the basic units of language. When a baby begins to speak, the way the excited mother reports what has happened is: 'Sally (or Tommy) has said her (or his) first word!' We would be surprised at a mother who described little Tommy's or Sally's first utterance as a sentence. Sentences come later, we are inclined to feel, when words are strung together meaningfully. That is not to say that a sentence must always consist of more than one word. One-word commands such as 'Go!' or 'Sit!', although they crop up relatively seldom in everyday conversation or reading, are not in any way odd or un-English. Nevertheless, learning to talk in early childhood seems to be a matter of putting words together, not of taking sentences apart.

There is a clear sense, then, in which words seem to be the building-blocks of language. Even as adults, there are quite a few circumstances in which we use single words outside the context of any actual or reconstructable sentence. Here are some examples:

- warning shouts, such as 'Fire!'
- conventional commands, such as 'Lights!', Camera!', 'Action!'
- items on shopping lists, such as 'carrots', 'cheese', 'eggs'.

It is clear also that words on their own, outside sentences, can be sorted and classified in various ways. A comprehensive classification of English words according to meaning is a thesaurus, such as *Roget's Thesaurus*. But the kind of conventional classification that we are likely to refer to most often is a dictionary, in which words are listed according to their spelling in alphabetical order.

Given that English spelling is so erratic, a common reason for looking up a word in an English dictionary is to check how to spell it. But another very common reason is to check what it means. In fact, that is what a dictionary entry basically consists of: an association of a word, alphabetically listed, with a definition of what it means, and perhaps also some information about grammar (the word class or part of speech that the word belongs to) and its pronunciation. Here, for example, is a specimen dictionary entry for the word *month*, based on the entry given in the *Concise Oxford Dictionary* (6th edition):

month *noun.* Any of twelve portions into which the year is divided.

It seems, then, that a word is not just a building-block of sentences: it is a building-block with a meaning that is unpredictable, or at least sufficiently unpredictable that learners of English, and even sometimes native speakers, may need to consult a dictionary in order to discover it.

We may be tempted to think that this constitutes everything that needs to be said about words: they are units of language which are basic in two senses, both

1. in that they have meanings that are unpredictable and so must be listed in dictionaries

and

2. in that they are the building-blocks out of which phrases and sentences are formed.

However, if that were all that needed to be said, this would be a very short book – much shorter than it actually is! So in what respects do 1. and 2. jointly fall short as a characterisation of words and their behaviour? A large part of the answer lies in the fact that there are units of language that have characteristic 1. but not 2., and vice versa. Sections 2.3 and 2.4 are devoted to demonstrating this. First, though, we will deal in Section 2.2 with a distinction which, though important, is independent of the distinctions that apply to words in particular.

2.2 Words as types and words as tokens

How many words are there in the following sentence?

(1) Mary goes to Edinburgh next week, and she intends going to Washington next month.

If we take as a guide the English spelling convention of placing a space between each word, the answer seems clearly to be fourteen. But there is also a sense in which there are fewer than fourteen words in the sentence, because two of them (the words *to* and *next*) are repeated. In this sense, the third word is the same as the eleventh, and the fifth word is the same as the thirteenth, so there are only twelve words in the sentence. Let us say that the third and the eleventh word of the sentence at (1) are distinct

tokens of a single **type**, and likewise the fifth and thirteenth word. (In much the same way, one can say that two performances of the same tune, or two copies of the same book, are distinct tokens of one type.) The type–token distinction is relevant to the notion 'word' in this way. Sentences (spoken or written) may be said to be composed of word-tokens, but it is clearly not word-tokens that are listed in dictionaries. It would be absurd to suggest that each occurrence of the word *next* in (1) merits a separate dictionary entry. Words as listed in dictionaries entries are, at one level, types, not tokens – even though, at another level, one may talk of distinct tokens of the same dictionary entry, inasmuch as the entry for *month* in one copy of the *Concise Oxford Dictionary* is a different token from the entry for *month* in another copy.

Is it enough, then, to say that characterisation 2. (words as building-blocks) relates to word-tokens and characterisation 1. (words as meaningful units) relates to word-types? Again, if that were all there was to it, this book could be quite short. The term *word* would be ambiguous between a 'type' interpretation and a 'token' interpretation; but the ambiguity would be just the same as is exhibited by many other terms not specifically related to language, such as *tune*: a tune I heard this morning may be 'the same' as one I heard yesterday (i.e. they may be instances of the same type), but the two tokens that I have heard of it are distinct. However, the relationship between words as building-blocks and as meaningful units is not so simple as that, as we shall see. So, while it is important to be alert to type–token ambiguity when talking about words, recognising this sort of ambiguity is by no means all there is to sorting out how characteristics 1. and 2. diverge.

2.3 Words with predictable meanings

Do any words have meanings that are predictable – that is, meanings that can be worked out on the basis of the sounds or combinations of sounds that make them up? (I consciously say 'sounds' rather than 'letters' because writing is secondary to speech: every normal human learns to speak, but it is only in the last century or so that a substantial proportion of the world's population has learned to read and write.) The answer is certainly 'yes', but not necessarily for reasons that immediately come to mind.

It is true that there are some words whose sound seems to reflect their meaning fairly directly. These include so-called **onomatopoeic** words, such as words for animal cries: *bow-wow, miaow, cheep, cock-a-doodle-doo*. But even here convention plays a large part. Onomatopoeic words are not the same in all languages; for example, a cock-crow in German is *kikeriki*, and a dog's bark in French is *ouah ouah* (pronounced roughly 'wah wah'). There are also sets of words in which some similarity in sound (say, in the cluster of consonants at the beginning) seems to reflect a vague similarity in meaning, such as smoothness or wetness or both in the set of words *slip, slop, slurp, slide, slither, sleek, slick, slaver, slug*. A technical term for this situation is **sound symbolism**. But in sound symbolism, quite apart from the role of convention, the sound–meaning relationship is even less direct than in onomatopoeia. The fact that a word begins with *sl-* does not guarantee that it has anything to do with smoothness or wetness (consider *slave, slit, slow*), and conversely there are many words that relate to smoothness and wetness but do not begin with *sl-*.

The idea that some words have meanings that are 'natural' or predictable in this way is really a leftover from childhood. Young children who have been exposed to only one language are often perplexed when they encounter a foreign language for the first time. 'Aren't *cat* and *dog* obviously the right words for those animals?', an English-speaking child may think; 'Why, then, do French people insist on calling them *chat* and *chien*?' Pretty soon, of course, everyone comes to realise that, in every language including their own, the associations between most words and their meanings are purely conventional. After all, if that were not so, the vocabularies of languages could not differ as much as they do. Even in onomatopoeia and sound symbolism this conventionality is still at work, so that people who know no English are unlikely to predict the meaning of *cock-a-doodle-doo* or *bow-wow* any more accurately than they can predict the meaning of *cat* or *dog*.

What kinds of word do have predictable meanings, then? The answer is: any words that are composed of independently identifiable parts, where the meaning of the parts is sufficient to determine the meaning of the whole word. Here is an example. Most readers of this book have probably never encountered the word *dioecious* (also spelled *diecious*), a botanical term meaning 'having male and female flowers on separate plants'. (It contrasts with *monoecious*, meaning 'having male and female flowers, or unisexual flowers, on the same plant'.) If you had been asked the meaning of the word *dioecious* before today, you would probably have had to look it up in the dictionary. Consider now sentence (2):

(2) Ginkgo trees reproduce dioeciously.

To work out what this sentence means, do you now need to look up *dioeciously* in a dictionary? It is, after all, another word that you are encountering here for the first time! Yet, knowing the meaning of *dioecious*, you will agree (I take it) that a dictionary is unnecessary. You can confidently predict that (2) means 'Ginkgo trees reproduce by means of male and female flowers on separate plants'. Your confidence is based on the fact that, knowing English, you know that the suffix -*ly* has a consistent meaning, so that *Xly* means 'in an X fashion', for any adjective X. Perhaps up to now you had not realised that you know this; but that merely reflects the fact that one's knowledge of one's native language is implicit, not explicit – at least until aspects of it are made explicit through schooling.

Dioeciously is an example of a word that, although not brand new (it may even be listed in some dictionaries), could just as well be brand new so far as most readers of this book are concerned. The fact that you could nevertheless understand it (once you had learned the meaning of *dioecious*, that is) suggests that you should have no difficulty using and understanding many words that really are brand new – words that no one has ever used before. It is easy to show that that is correct. Here are three sentences containing words that, so far as I know, had never been used by anyone before my use of them today, in the year 2000:

(3) Vice-President Gore is likely to use deliberately un-Clintonish electioneering tactics.

(4) It will be interesting to see how quickly President Putin de-Yeltsinises the Russian government.

(5) The current emphasis on rehabilitative goals in judicial punishment may give rise to an antirehabilitationist reaction among people who place more weight on retribution and deterrence.

You will have no difficulty interpreting these sentences. Un-Clintonish tactics are tactics unlike those that President Clinton would use, and a de-Yeltsinised government is one purged of the influence of Boris Yeltsin. The word *antirehabilitationist* may strike you as ugly or cumbersome, but its meaning is likewise clear. In fact, it is virtually inevitable that words with predictable meanings should exist, given that English vocabulary changes over time. If one examines words that first came into use in the twentieth century, one will certainly encounter some that appear from nowhere, so to speak, with meanings that are unguessable from their shape, such as *jazz* or *gizmo*. The vast majority, however, are words whose meanings, if not strictly predictable, are at any rate motivated in the sense that they can be reliably guessed by someone who encounters them for the first time in an appropriate context. Examples are *computer* or *quadraphonic* or *gentrification*, all of which have meanings that are sufficiently unpredictable to require listing in any up-to-date dictionary, but none of which would have been totally opaque to an adult English-speaker encountering them when they were first used.

What these examples show is that one of the characteristics suggested in Section 2.1 as applicable to all words – that they have meanings that are unpredictable and so must be listed in dictionaries – is not after all totally general. If *dioecious* and *rehabilitation* are listed, then *dioeciously* and *antirehabilitationist* do not need to be listed as well, at least not if semantic unpredictability is the criterion. And a novel word such as *un-Clintonish* is perfectly understandable even though the base from which it is formed is a proper name (*Clinton*) and hence will not be listed in most dictionaries. The link between wordhood, semantic unpredictability and dictionary listing is thus less close than you may at first have thought. In Exercise 1 at the end of this chapter you will find further examples of words whose meanings are predictable, alongside words of similar shape whose meaning certainly cannot be guessed.

Is it, then, that the common view of words as basic semantic building-blocks of language is simply wrong? That would be too sweeping. What examples such as *computer* illustrate is that a word's meaning may be motivated (a computer is certainly used, among other things, for computing, that is for performing calculations) but nevertheless idiosyncratic (it is not the case, in the early twenty-first century, that anyone or anything that performs calculations can be called a computer). In some instances a word's original motivation is totally obscured by its pronunciation but can still be glimpsed from its spelling, as with *cupboard* and *handkerchief*. It is as if words are intrinsically prone to drift semantically, and in particular to acquire meanings that are more specialised than one would predict if one had never encountered them before. Why this should be is a large question, still not fully answered, involving the study of linguistic semantics, of language change, and of how knowledge about words is acquired and stored in the brain. For present purposes, what matters is to be aware that not every word can be listed in a dictionary, even in the fullest dictionary imaginable.

2.4 Non-words with unpredictable meanings

In Section 2.3 we saw that it is possible for a linguistic item to be a basic building-block of syntax – that is, an item that is clearly not itself a sentence or a phrase – and yet to have a meaning that is predictable. We saw, in other words, that characteristic 2. does not necessarily entail characteristic 1. In this section we will see that characteristic 1. does not necessarily entail characteristic 2.: that is, something that is clearly larger than a word (being composed of two or more words) may nevertheless have a meaning that is not entirely predictable from the meanings of the words that compose it.

Consider these two sentences from the point of view of a learner of English who is familiar with the usual meanings of the words *expenditure*, *note* and *tab*:

(6) I keep notes on all my expenditure.
(7) I keep tabs on all my expenditure.

Will this learner be able to interpret both these sentences accurately? The answer, surely, is no. Sentence (6) presents no problem; the learner should be able to interpret it correctly as meaning 'I write down a record of everything I spend'. But faced with sentence (7), on the basis of the usual meaning of *tab*, the learner is likely to be puzzled. Does it mean something like 'I attach small flaps to all the notes and coins that I spend'? Or perhaps 'I tear off small pieces from the paper money that I spend, and keep them'? Neither interpretation makes much sense! Native speakers of English, however, will have no difficulty with (7). They will instinctively interpret *keep tabs on* as a single unit, meaning 'pay close attention to' or 'monitor carefully'. Thus, *keep tabs on*, although it consists of three words, functions as a single unit semantically, its meaning not being predictable from that of these three words individually. In technical terms, *keep tabs on* is an **idiom**. Even though it is not a word, it will appear in any dictionary that takes seriously the task of listing semantic idiosyncrasies, probably under the headword *tab*.

Idioms are enormously various in length, structure and function. *Keep tabs on* behaves rather like a verb, as do *take a shine to* 'become attracted to', *raise Cain* 'create a disturbance', *have a chip on one's shoulder* 'be resentful', and *kick the bucket* 'die'. Many idioms behave more like nouns, as the following pair of sentences illustrates:

(8) The interrogation took a long time because the suspect kept introducing irrelevant arguments.
(9) The interrogation took a long time because the suspect kept introducing red herrings.

Again, a learner of English might be puzzled by (9): did the suspect keep pulling fish from his pocket? A native speaker, however, will know that *red herring* is an idiom meaning 'irrelevant argument', so that (8) and (9) mean the same thing. Other noun-like idioms are *white elephant* 'unwanted object', *dark horse* 'competitor whose strength is unknown', *Aunt Sally* 'target of mockery'.

In most of the idioms that we have looked at so far, all the individual words (*tabs, shine, bucket, elephant* etc.) have a literal or non-idiomatic meaning in other contexts. Even in *raise Cain*, the fact that *Cain* is spelled with a capital letter hints at a reference to the elder son of Adam, who, according to biblical legend, murdered his younger brother Abel. However, there are also words that never occur except in an idiomatic context. Consider these examples:

(10) My aunt took pains to get the answer right.
(11) My aunt took part in the conversation.
(12) My aunt took offence at the suggestion.
(13) My aunt took umbrage at the suggestion.

(10), (11) and (12), *take pains*, *take part* and *take offence* all deserve to be called idioms, because they are multi-word items whose meaning is not fully predictable from their component words. (To a learner of English, (11) might seem to imply that my aunt was present during only part of the conversation, and (12) might suggest that she committed an offence.) If so, then presumably we should say the same of (13), containing the phrase *take umbrage at*. The difference between (13) and the others, however, is that *umbrage* does not appear anywhere except in this phrase (in my usage, at least). This restriction means that it would not really be sufficient for a dictionary to list *umbrage* as a noun meaning something like 'annoyance'; rather, what needs to be listed is the whole phrase. Similarly, the word *cahoots* exists only in the phrase *in cahoots with* 'in collusion with', and it is the whole phrase which deserves to be lexically listed, as an idiom.

Akin to idioms, but distinguishable from them, are phrases in which individual words have **collocationally restricted** meanings. Consider the following phrases:

(14) white wine
(15) white coffee
(16) white noise
(17) white man

Semantically, these phrases are by no means totally idiosyncratic: they denote a kind of wine, coffee, noise and man, respectively. Nevertheless, in a broad sense they may count as idiomatic, because the meaning that *white* has in them is not its usual meaning; rather, when collocated with *wine*, *coffee*, *noise* and *man* respectively, it has the meanings 'yellow', 'brown (with milk)' (at least in British usage), 'containing many frequencies with about equal amplitude', and 'belonging to an ethnic group whose members' skin colour is typically pinkish or pale brown'.

If a typical idiom is a phrase, then a word with a collocationally restricted meaning is smaller than a typical idiom. That provokes the question whether there are linguistic items with unpredictable meanings that are larger than phrases – specifically, that constitute whole sentences. The answer is yes: many **proverbs** fall into this category. A proverb is a traditional saying, syntactically a sentence, whose conventional interpretation differs from what is suggested by the literal meaning of the words it contains. Examples are:

(18) Too many cooks spoil the broth.
      'Having too may people involved in a task makes it harder to complete.'
(19) A stitch in time saves nine.
      'Anticipating a future problem and taking care to avoid it is less troublesome in the long run than responding to the problem after it has arisen.'
(20) It's no use crying over spilt milk.
      'After an accident one should look to the future, rather than waste time wishing the accident had not happened.'

Here again, it is useful to distinguish between predictability and motivation. The relationship between the literal meaning and the conventional interpretation of these proverbs is not totally arbitrary. Rather, the conventional interpretation is motivated in the sense that it arises through metaphorical extension of the literal meaning. For example, spilling milk is one kind of accident, but in the proverb at (20) it is used metaphorically to stand for any accident. However, idioms are still unpredictable in the sense of being conventional; for example, one cannot freely invent a new idiom such as 'It's no use crying over a broken plate', even though its metaphorical meaning may be just as clear as that of (20).

If idioms are listed in dictionaries (usually via one of the words that they contain), should proverbs be listed too? As it happens, ordinary dictionaries do not usually list proverbs, because they are conventionally regarded as belonging not to the vocabulary of a language but to its usage (a rather vague term for kinds of linguistic convention that lie outside grammar). For present purposes, what is important about proverbs is that they constitute a further example of a linguistic unit whose use and meaning are in some degree unpredictable, but which is larger than a word.

2.5 Conclusion: words versus lexical items

Section 2.1 pointed out that we tend to think of words as possessing two characteristics: 1. they have meanings that are unpredictable and so must be listed in dictionaries, and 2. they are the building-blocks for words and phrases. In Sections 2.3 and 2.4 I have argued that, although this may be broadly true, the two characteristics do not always go together. For this reason, it will be helpful to have distinct terms for items with each of the two characteristics. Let us use **lexical item** for items with characteristic 1., and reserve **word** for items with characteristic 2. (Admittedly, characteristic 2. is formulated quite vaguely; however, making the formulation more precise belongs not to a book on word-formation but to a book on syntax.)What we have seen in Section 2.3 is that there are some words that are not lexical items, while Section 2.4 has shown that there are some lexical items that are not words.

Does this show that the traditional view of words as things that are (or should be) listed in dictionaries is entirely wrong? Not really. I have already pointed out in Section 2.3 that, although many words have meanings that are predictable, there is nevertheless a tendency for these meanings to lose motivation over time. Thus a word which does not start out as a lexical item may in due course become one. (This tendency will be discussed again in Chapter 5.) Conversely, many of the lexical items that are phrases or sentences (idioms or proverbs) have meanings which can be seen as metaphorical extensions of a literal meaning; so to that extent their interpretation remains motivated.

Given that there is not a perfect match between words and lexical items, which should dictionaries list? Or should they list both? The practice of most dictionaries reflects a compromise. Some are more generous than others in listing idioms; some are more generous than others in listing words with entirely predictable meanings. For readers of this book, the important thing is to be aware that there are two distinct kinds of item that a dictionary may seek to list, and that this implicit conflict may help to explain apparently puzzling decisions that dictionary editors make about what to include and what to leave out.

Exercises

1. Which of the following words may *not* deserve to be regarded as lexical items, and so may not need to be listed in a dictionary of modern English? Why?

a.	break	breaking	breakable	breakage
	read	reading	readable	
	punish	punishing	punishable	punishment
b.	conceive		conceivable	conception
	receive	receptive	receivable	reception
	perceive	perceptive	perceivable	perception
c.	gregarious	gregariousness	gregariously	
	happy	happiness	happily	
	high	highness	highly	

2. Construct further sets of words similar to those in Exercise 1, and try to distinguish between the words that deserve to be recognised as lexical items and those that do not, giving your reasons.

3. Using a large dictionary that gives the dates when each word was first recorded (such as *The New Shorter Oxford English Dictionary* or *The Random House Dictionary of the English Language*), find five words that were first used in the twentieth century. How many of them have meanings that would have been guessable by an adult English speaker on first encounter, and how many do not?

4. Which of the following phrases (in italics) may deserve to be regarded as lexical items? Why? (If you are not a native speaker of English, you may like to consult a native speaker about what these sentences mean.)

a. They *put the cat among the hamsters*.
b. They *put the cat among the pigeons*.
c. They *put out* the cat before going to bed.
d. They *put out* the light before going to bed.
e. They really *put themselves out* for us.
f. They looked really *put out*.
g. Roger is *a man who keeps his promises*.
h. Richard is *a man of his word*.
i. *A man in the road* witnessed the accident.
j. *The man in the street* is not interested in economic policy.
k. Rupert is *a man about town*.
l. I met *a man with an umbrella*.
m. May *the best man* win.
n. *The best man* unfortunately lost the rings on the way to the wedding.

5. Look up the following words in two or three medium-sized dictionaries:

unperplexed   sensitiveness   poorish   de-urbanise

Is their existence recorded, and, if so, how? For any whose existence is not recorded, does the dictionary supply suitable information for a non-English-speaker to work out its meaning?

Recommendations for reading

On onomatopoeia and sound symbolism, see Marchand (1969), chapter 7, Jakobson and Waugh (1979), chapter 4, and Hinton, Nichols and Ohala (1994).

My discussion of the distinction between words as grammatical units and lexical items owes much to Di Sciullo and Williams (1987), chapter 1. This book as a whole presupposes considerable knowledge of linguistic theory, but chapter 1 can be read without it. For what I call 'lexical items', they use the term 'listemes'.

The relationship of clichés and idioms to other aspects of linguistic knowledge is discussed by Jackendoff (1997).

3 A word and its parts: roots, affixes and their shapes

3.1 Taking words apart

We saw in Chapter 2 that there are many words that need not be listed in dictionaries, because their meanings are completely predictable (such as *dioeciously*), and many which cannot be listed, simply because they may never have been used (such as *un-Clintonish* and *antirehabilitationist*). These are all words which are not lexical items. But what is the basis of their semantic predictability? It must be that these unlisted and unlistable words are composed of identifiable smaller parts (at least two), put together in a systematic fashion so that the meaning of the whole word can be reliably determined. In *un-Clintonish* these smaller parts are clearly *un-*, *Clinton* and *-ish*; in *dioeciously* these parts include *dioecious* and *-ly*, with further smaller components being perhaps discernible within *dioecious*. In this chapter we will focus on these smaller parts of words, generally called **morphemes**. (The area of grammar concerned with the structure of words and with relationships between words involving the morphemes that compose them is technically called **morphology**, from the Greek word *morphe* 'form, shape'; and morphemes can be thought of as the minimal units of morphology.) In Sections 3.2 and 3.3 we will be concerned with two important distinctions between different kinds of morpheme, and in Section 3.4 we will consider ways in which a morpheme can vary in shape.

Before we embark on those issues, however, there is an important point to be made concerning the distinction between words that are lexical items and words that are not. As we have seen, words that are not lexical items must be complex, in the sense that they are composed of two or more morphemes. But those are not the only words that are complex; lexical-item words can be complex too – in fact, we encountered many such examples in the exercises to Chapter 2. To put it another way: words that are lexical items do not have to be **monomorphemic** (consisting of just one morpheme). This is hardly surprising, when one considers that we have already encountered lexical items that are so complex as to extend over more than one word, namely idioms. But recognising the existence of lexical items that are **polymorphemic** (consisting of more than one morpheme) has an important bearing on the relationship between morphemes and meaning, as we shall see.

Let us look in more detail at two characteristics of morphemes, in the light of how the notion has been introduced. To allow the meanings of some complex words to be predictable, morphemes must

1. be identifiable from one word to another

and

2. contribute in some way to the meaning of the whole word.

Now, what permits the same morpheme to be identified in a variety of different words? A morpheme cannot, after all, be just any recurring word-part. To see this, consider the words *attack*, *stack*, *tackle* and *taxi*. These all contain a syllable pronounced like the word *tack*; but it would be absurd to say that the same morpheme *-tack-* is identifiable in each, because the meaning of *tack* has nothing to do with the meanings of the other words, and all of them must surely be listed separately in any dictionary. So it may seem natural to link characteristic 1. tightly to 2., making the identification of morphemes dependent on their meaning. Indeed, in introductory linguistics textbooks, one often encounters statements to the effect that morphemes are not merely the smallest units of grammatical structure but also the smallest meaningful units. This view is widespread precisely because it fits many complex words very well – not only brand new words like *un-Clintonish* but also established words like *helpfulness*, which is divisible into the morphemes *help*, *-ful* (identifiable also in *cheerful* and *doleful*, for example) and *-ness* (identifiable also in *happiness* and *sadness*). It seems reasonable to say that the meaning of both *un-Clintonish* and *helpfulness* is entirely determined by the meanings of the morphemes that they contain. Even the meaning of a word such as *readable*, which (as we saw in Exercise 1 of Chapter 2) is idiosyncratic enough to require mention in a dictionary, is clearly related to the normal meanings or functions of *read* and *-able*. In the face of such examples, it is important to remember that there is no necessary or logical connection between characteristics 1. and 2. Repeatedly in the following sections, but especially in Section 3.5, we will encounter evidence that it is risky to tie the identification of morphemes too closely to their meaning.

Another general point to be made about morphemes is that, although they are the parts out of which words are composed, they do not have to be of any particular length. Some relatively long words, such as *catamaran* and *knickerbocker*, may consist of just one morpheme; on the other hand, a single-syllable word, such as *tenths*, may contain as many as three morphemes (*ten*, *-th*, *-s*). What this shows is that the morphological structure of words is largely independent of their **phonological** structure (their division into sounds, syllables and rhythmic units). This reflects a striking difference between human speech and all animal communication systems: only speech (so far as we know) is analysable in two parallel ways, into units that contribute to meaning (morphemes, words, phrases etc.) and units that are individually meaningless (sounds, syllables etc.). The implications of this property of human language (its so-called **duality of patterning**) go way beyond the scope of this book. What matters here is just that you should avoid a mistake that beginners sometimes make, that of confusing morphemes with phonological units such as syllables.

3.2 Kinds of morpheme: bound versus free

The morphemes in the word *helpfulness*, just discussed, do not all have the same status. *Help*, *-ful* and *-ness* are not simply strung together like beads on a string. Rather, the core, or starting-point, for the formation of this word is *help*; the morpheme *-ful* is then added to form *helpful*, which in turn is the basis for the formation of *helpfulness*. In using the word 'then' here, I am not referring to the historical sequence in which the words *help*, *helpful* and *helpfulness* came into use; I am talking rather about the structure of the word in contemporary English – a structure that is part of the implicit linguistic knowledge of all English speakers, whether or not they know anything about the history of the English language.

There are two reasons for calling *help* the core of this word. One is that *help* supplies the most precise and concrete element in its meaning, shared by a family of related words like *helper*, *helpless*, *helplessness* and *unhelpful* that differ from one another in more abstract ways. (This is an aspect of word structure that we will look at in more detail in Chapter 5.) Another reason is that, of the three morphemes in *helpfulness*, only *help* can stand on its own – that is, only *help* can, in an appropriate context, constitute an utterance by itself. That is clearly not true of *-ness*, nor is it true of *-ful*. (Historically *-ful* is indeed related to the word *full*, but their divergence in modern English is evident if one compares words like *helpful* and *cheerful* with other words that really do contain *full*, such as *half-full* and *chock-full*.) In self-explanatory fashion, morphemes that can stand on their own are called **free**, and ones that cannot are **bound**.

A salient characteristic of English – a respect in which English differs from many other languages – is that a high proportion of complex words are like *helpfulness* and *un-Clintonish* in that they have a free morpheme (like *help* and *Clinton*) at their core. Compare the two column of words listed at (1), all of which consist uncontroversially of two morphemes, separated by a hyphen:

(1)   a.   read-able   b.   leg-ible
                   hear-ing   audi-ence
                   en-large   magn-ify
                   perform-ance   rend-ition
                   white-ness   clar-ity
                   dark-en   obfusc-ate
                   seek-er   applic-ant

The rationale for the division is that the words in column a. all contain a free morpheme, respectively *read, hear, large, perform, white* and *dark*. By contrast, in the words in column b., though they are similar in meaning to their counterparts in a., both the morphemes are bound. If you know something about the history of the English language, or if you know some French, Spanish or Latin, you may know already that most of the free morphemes in (1a) belong to that part of the vocabulary of English that has been inherited directly through the Germanic branch of the Indo-European language family to which English belongs, whereas all the morphemes in (1b) have been introduced, or borrowed, from Latin, either directly or via French. We will return to these historical matters in Chapter 9. Even without such historical knowledge, it may strike you that the words in (1b) are on the whole somewhat less common, or more bookish, than those in (1a). This reflects the fact that, among the most widely used words, the Germanic element still predominates. It is thus fair to say that, in English, there is still a strong tendency for complex words to contain a free morpheme at their core.

Is it possible for a bound morpheme to be so limited in its distribution that it occurs in just one complex word? The answer is yes. This is almost true, for example, of the morpheme *leg-* 'read' in *legible* at (1b): at least in everyday vocabulary, it is found in only one other word, namely *illegible*, the negative counterpart of *legible*. And it is absolutely true of the morphemes *cran-, huckle-* and *gorm-* in *cranberry, huckleberry* and *gormless*. *Cranberry* and *huckleberry* are compounds (a kind of complex word to be discussed in Chapter 6) whose second element is clearly the free morpheme *berry*, occurring in several other compounds such as *straw-berry, blackberry* and *blueberry*; however, *cran-* and *huckle-* occur nowhere outside these compounds. A name commonly given to such bound morphemes is **cranberry morpheme**. Cranberry morphemes are more than just a curiosity, because they reinforce the difficulty of tying morphemes tightly to meaning. What does *cran-* mean? Arguably, nothing at all; it is only the entire word *cranberry* that can be said to be meaningful, and it is certainly the entire word, not *cran-* by itself, that is in any dictionary. (You may have noticed, too, that although blackberries are indeed blackish, strawberries have nothing obvious to do with straw; so, even if *straw-* in *strawberry* is not a cranberry morpheme, it does not by itself make any predictable semantic contribution in this word.)

3.3 Kinds of morpheme: root, affix, combining form

In Section 3.2 I have used the term 'core of a word' in a rather vague way, to denote the morpheme that makes the most precise and concrete contribution to the word's meaning. I have also refrained so far from using two terms that may be already familiar to you: prefix and suffix. It is time now to bring those two terms into the discussion, and also introduce the term **root** for what I have been calling the 'core'.

From Section 3.2 it emerged that, in the native Germanic portion of the vocabulary, the root of a complex word is usually free. Of the non-root morphemes in the words that we have looked at so far, those that precede the root (like *en-* in *enlarge*) are called **prefixes**, while those that follow it are called **suffixes** (like *-ance* in *performance*, *-ness* in *whiteness*, and *-able* in *readable*). We have encountered far more suffixes than prefixes, and that is not an accident: there are indeed more suffixes than prefixes in English. An umbrella term for prefixes and suffixes (broadly speaking, for all morphemes that are not roots) is **affix**.

Only root morphemes can be free, so affixes are necessarily bound. We have already noticed that the morphemes *-ful* and *-ness* of *helpfulness* cannot stand on their own. It is easy for anyone who is a native speaker of English to check that the same is true of all the morphemes that I have identified as prefixes and suffixes in (1a) – that is, all the morphemes in these words other than the roots.

At this point, it may seem to some readers that terminology is proliferating unnecessarily. If affixes are always bound, do not 'bound morpheme' and 'affix' mean essentially the same thing? Likewise, if roots are usually free, do we really need both the terms 'root' and 'free morpheme'? The answer lies in the word 'usually' in the previous sentence. Affixes are indeed always bound, but it is not the case that roots are always free. In fact, all the words in (1b) have roots that are bound. The fact of being bound may make a bound root harder to identify and isolate as a morpheme than a free root is; but for most of the examples in (1b) it is possible to find other words in which the same roots appear, such as *audible, auditory* and *audition* alongside *audience*. A cranberry morpheme can be thought of as a bound root that occurs in only one word.

We have so far encountered two main kinds of complex word: ones with a single free root, as in (1a), and ones with a single bound root, as in (1b). Is it the case, then, that a word can contain no more than one root? Certainly not – indeed, such words are very common; they are **compounds**, already mentioned in connection with cranberry morphemes. Examples are *bookcase, motorbike, penknife, truck-driver*. The point of mentioning compounds again now is that, if a complex word can be formed out of two (or more) free roots, it is natural to ask whether a word can contain two or more bound roots. The answer is yes – although, in the light of the English language's preference for free roots, they are not nearly so common as ordinary compounds. Examples of words with two bound roots are *electrolysis, electroscopy, microscopy, microcosm, pachyderm, echinoderm*. Other words which, like *cranberry*, contain one bound and one free root are *microfilm, electrometer* and *Sino-Japanese* (assuming that *Japanese* contains the free root *Japan*). It will be evident straight away that these are mostly not words in common use; in fact, I would expect few readers of this book to be familiar with all of them. Unlike ordinary compounds, these words are nearly all technical terms of scientific vocabulary, coined self-consciously out of non-English elements, mostly from Latin and Greek. Because of the big difference between ordinary compounds and these learned words, and because of the non-English character of the bound morphemes that compose them, many linguists and dictionary-makers classify these bound morphemes as neither affixes nor bound roots (such as we encountered in (1b)) but place them in a special category of **combining forms**.

Given that native English words generally contain free roots, we might expect that, if a word made up of combining forms is in common use, the morphemes within it should tend to acquire the status of free morphemes. This expectation turns out to be correct. For example, the word *photograph* existed, as a learned technical term composed of combining forms, before the word *photo*, but *photo* must now be classified as a free morpheme. Other combining forms that have more recently 'acquired their freedom' are *micro-* and *macro-* (as in *at a micro level* or *on a macro scale*) and *retro-*, as applied to music or fashion.

3.4 Morphemes and their allomorphs

Is every morpheme pronounced the same in all contexts? If it were, most phonology texts could be considerably shorter than they are! In fact, many morphemes have two or more different pronunciations, called **allomorphs**, the choice between them being determined by the context. These include some of the commonest morphemes in the language, as I will illustrate directly. I will then discuss in more detail what aspects of the context can influence the choice of allomorph.

How are the plurals of most English nouns formed? If one compares *cats, dogs* and *horses* with *cat, dog* and *horse* respectively, the obvious answer is: 'by adding -*s*'. But English spelling is notoriously unreliable as a guide to pronunciation. In fact, this -*s* suffix has three allomorphs: [s] (as in *cats* or *lamps*), [z] (as in *dogs* or *days*), and [ɪz] or [əz] (as in *horses* or *judges*). Is it, then, that everyone learning English, whether natively or as a second language, must learn individually for each noun which of the three allomorphs is used in its plural form? That would seem extremely laborious. In fact, it is easy to show that the three allomorphs are distributed in an entirely regular fashion, based on the sound immediately preceding the suffix, thus:

• when the preceding sound is a sibilant (the kind of 'hissing' or 'hushing' sound heard at the end of *horse, rose, bush, church* and *judge*), the [ɪz] allomorph occurs
• otherwise, when the preceding sound is voiceless, i.e. produced with no vibration of the vocal folds in the larynx (as in *cat, rock, cup* or *cliff*), the [s] allomorph occurs
• otherwise (i.e. after a vowel or a voiced consonant, as in *dog* or *day*), the [z] allomorph occurs.

In effect, without realising it, we pay attention to these phonological characteristics of the noun when deciding which allomorph to use – though 'decide' is hardly the right word here, because our 'decision' is quite unconscious. Another very common suffix with phonologically determined allomorphs is the one spelled -*ed*, used in the past tense form of most verbs. Its allomorphs are [t], [d] and [ɪd] or [əd]; determining their distribution is left as an exercise, whose solution is provided at the end of the book.

One may be tempted to think that the **allomorphy** involved here (i.e. the choice of allomorphs), because it depends so much on phonology, is not really a morphological matter at all. But that is not quite correct. Consider the noun *lie* meaning 'untruth'. Its plural form is *lies*, with [z] – just as predicted, given that *lie* ends in a vowel sound. But this is not because either [s] or [əz] would be unpronounceable here, or would break some rule of English phonology. If we experiment by replacing the [z] of *lies* with [s], we get an actual word (*lice*, the plural of *louse*), and replacing it with [əz] we get what is at least a possible word (it might be the plural of an imaginary noun '*lia*') – and is an actual word (*liars*) in those dialects of English where *liar* is pronounced without an *r*-sound. So phonologically determined allomorphy need not just be a matter of avoiding what is phonologically prohibited.

It is not only phonology that may influence the choice of allomorphs of a morpheme. Instances where grammar or vocabulary play a part in the choice are extremely numerous in English. In this book we will do no more than skim the surface of this huge topic. We will look first at a set of examples that involve both grammar and vocabulary, before showing in Section 3.5 how a morpheme's peculiar allomorphy can be crucial in establishing its existence.

The words *laugh* and *cliff* both end in the same voiceless consonant (despite what the spelling may suggest!). Therefore, according to the formula given above, the allomorph of the plural suffix that appears on them should be [s]. And this is correct. But what about *wife* and *loaf*? These end in the same voiceless consonant as *laugh* and *cliff*; yet their plurals are not **wifes* and **loafs* but *wives* and *loaves*. (The asterisk is a conventional symbol to indicate that a linguistic expression (a word, phrase or sentence) is unacceptable for some reason to do with grammar or with the structure of the language generally, rather than for reasons such as truthfulness or politeness.) In fact, there are quite a few nouns which, in the singular, end in a voiceless *f*, *s* or *th* sound but which change this in the plural to the voiced counterpart (not always reflected in the spelling). Nouns that behave like this in most varieties of English are *knives, lives, hooves, houses, paths* and *baths*. However, there are also exceptions to this 'rule': apart from *laugh* and *cliff*, already mentioned, one can think of *fife* and *oaf*, which both form their plural with [s]. What's more, *wife, knife* and the rest do not use their voiced allomorph (*wive-* etc.) before any morpheme except plural -*s* – not even before the 'apostrophe *s*' morpheme that indicates possession, as in *my wife's job*. So the allomorphy here is determined both lexically (it is restricted to certain nouns only) and grammatically (it occurs before the plural suffix -*s* but not before other morphemes). This state of affairs suggests a refinement to the bound-free distinction: as a morpheme, *wife* is clearly free, but, of its two allomorphs *wife* (with final [f]) and *wive* (with final [v]), only the former is free, while the latter is bound.

3.5 Identifying morphemes independently of meaning

A somewhat different kind of lexical conditioning can be introduced by means of the prefix *re-* and its possible allomorphs. This prefix can be added to verbs quite freely, contributing the meaning 'again', as in *rewrite*, *reread, repaint, revisit.* In these words the prefix has a vowel rather like that of *see*, and can be represented phonetically as [ri]. But something that looks very much like the same prefix occurs also in verbs such as *revive, return, restore, revise, reverse*, this time pronounced with a so-called 'reduced vowel', [rɪ] or [rə]. What's more, many of these words have a meaning in which it is possible to discern an element such as 'again' or 'backward movement': for example, *revive* means 'bring back to life', *return* means 'come back' or 'give back', *restore* means 'bring back to a former condition', and *revise* means 'look at again, with a view to changing'. It may therefore seem natural to treat [ri] and [rə] as allomorphs of the same morpheme.

A snag, however, is that there are some roots with which both [ri] and [rə] can occur, yielding different meanings: for example, the meanings just given for *restore* and *return* are distinct from those for *re-store* 'store again' and *re-turn* 'turn again' (as in *I turned the steaks on the barbecue a minute ago, and I'll re-turn them soon*). The [ri] prefix can be added to almost any verb, with the consistent meaning 'again' (it is productive in all the senses to be discussed in Chapter 8), whereas the [rə] prefix is lexically much more restricted as well as harder to pin down semantically. One must conclude that the two prefixes pronounced [ri] and [rə] belong to distinct morphemes in modern English, their phonetic and semantic similarities being due to their having the same historical source in that part of English vocabulary that has been borrowed from Latin via French.

As an alternative to that conclusion, one might consider rejecting the analysis of *revive, return, restore, revise* and *reverse* as consisting of a prefix plus a root, and instead treat them as monomorphemic. But this has unwelcome consequences too. If *revive* and *revise* are single morphemes, that amounts to saying that they have no parts in common (except phonologically) with *survive* and *supervise*. But that is unwelcome, because it inhibits us from recognising *sur-* and *super-* as morphemes that recur in *surpass* and *superimpose*. In fact, many English words (mainly verbs and words related to them) form a complex network, with what looks like a prefix–root structure (the root being usually bound), but without any clear consistent meaning being ascribable to either the prefix or the root. Here is just a small part of that network:

(2) | refer | prefer | confer | defer | transfer | infer |
reduce		conduce	deduce		induce
revoke		convoke			invoke
reserve	preserve	conserve	deserve		
relate		collate		translate	

remit		commit		transmit	
	pretend	contend			intend
revolve			devolve		involve

If we adhere strictly to the view that individual morphemes must be meaningful, then all these words must seemingly be treated as monomorphemic; for no consistent meaning can be identified in modern English for any of the purported morphemes that they contain (for example, no element such as 'backward movement' or 'again' can be plausibly discerned within the meaning of *reserve*). But a consideration of allomorphy shows that that would be unsatisfactory. If *reduce, conduce, deduce* and *induce* have no morpheme in common, then the fact that for all of them there is a corresponding noun in which -*duce* is replace with -*duct*- (*reduction, conduction* etc.) seems to be a pure accident. However, this shared pattern of allomorphy is just what we expect if -*duce* is a root morpheme that they all share (one of its allomorphs being -*duct*-), while they differ prefixally. A similar point can be made about the nouns *revolution, devolution* and *involution* related to *revolve, devolve* and *involve*: again, an unusual pattern of allomorphy makes sense if the same root morpheme is contained in all these words (-*volve*, with allomorph -*volu*-), but it makes no sense if these words have no more in common than e.g. *loaf* and *oaf*, discussed in Section 3.4.

Some of the nouns and verbs that I have just claimed to be related do not have much to do with each other semantically, one must admit. For example, the meaning of *conduce* (a rather rare verb) has nothing to do with that of *conduction*, and the noun that seems most closely related to *involve* is not *involution* (another rarity) but *involvement*. However, that just confirms a central characteristic of these prefix–root combinations: the prefixes and roots that they comprise are identifiable without reference to meaning. Because of this, all these complex words must clearly be lexical items. Thus the lexical conditioning to which these morphemes are subject is of a particularly strong kind: none of them ever occurs except in complex words that require dictionary listing.

The idea that these morphemes occur only in words that are lexical items fits nicely a salient characteristic of the table at (2), namely its 'gappiness'. A list of lexical items is essentially arbitrary; therefore one will not expect to be able to predict confidently that any one conceivable prefix–root combination will be present in the list. For example, nothing guarantees that there should be a word such as '*transvoke*' or '*premit*' – and indeed there is not (at least in the ordinary vocabulary of modern English speakers). Two of the gaps in (2) might be filled if we allowed as fillers not just verbs but other words related to them: for, even though '*transduce*' and '*convolve*' do not exist, we can find *transducer, convolution* and *convoluted* in any dictionary. It may seem at first paradoxical that these other words should exist while the verbs from which they are formed, in some sense (the sense in which e.g. *helpful* is 'formed from' *help*), do not exist. Again, however, this ceases to be surprising if the Latin-derived prefixes and roots that we have been considering have so extensively lost any clearly identifiable meanings as to enforce lexical listing for all words formed with them.

3.6 Conclusion: ways of classifying word-parts

It was argued in Chapter 2 that many words are divisible into parts. Chapter 3 has been concerned with classifying these parts, and discussing further their relation to word-meanings. We have introduced the following distinctions:

* morphemes and allomorphs, bound and free
* roots, affixes and combining forms
* prefixes and suffixes.

Allomorphy, concerned as it is with differences in how a morpheme is pronounced, may seem at first to have little connection with meaning. But in Section 3.6 we saw that allomorphy does have a role in the identification of morphemes, and hence in the issue of whether a word should be regarded as polymorphemic or not, despite the lack of clearcut meanings for the morphemes concerned.

I hope to have persuaded readers to be wary of definitions of the term 'morpheme' that refer to it as a unit of meaning. At the same time, one must acknowledge that, in large swathes of English vocabulary (in words such as *unhelpfulness*, *un-Clintonish* or *de-Yeltsinise*, for example) a close relationship between morphemes and meaning is discernible. In fact, one of the most prominent features of English vocabulary as it has accumulated over the centuries (one of its chief glories, in the eyes of many scholars and writers) is the existence both of words in which morphological structure and meaning seem closely associated, and of many words in which the relationship is obscure. The availability of these two elements in English vocabulary helps to make possible a kind of stylistic variety in English writing which is hard to match in languages where word-structure is more uniform.

Exercises

Consider the following words:

(a) tigers	(b) untimely	(c) decorating
speakers	uniquely	decentralising
(d) wholesome	(e) consumed	(f) leucocyte
gruesome	consumption	erythrocyte

1. Divide them into morphemes, noting any instances where you are unsure. What differences are there between the words in each pair?
2. Are there any morphemes here which have two or more allomorphs?
3. Which of these morphemes are free and which are bound? Are the bound morphemes all affixes, or are some of them roots or combining forms?
4. Do any problems arise here for the view that morphemes are 'the smallest units of language that can be associated with meaning' or 'the minimal units of meaning'?
5. In this chapter it was claimed that the words in (1b) all contain bound roots. Can any of these roots be seen as bound allomorphs of a morpheme that also has a free allomorph? And are any of these roots cranberry morphemes?
6. What phonological factors determine the distribution of the allomorphs [t], [d], and [ɪd] or [əd] of the past tense suffix -ed? ('Two of the factors are the same as for the plural suffix -s, but one is different.)

Recommendations for reading

For further discussion of the basic concepts 'morpheme', 'allomorph', 'affix' etc., consult an introductory text such as Bauer (1988), Matthews (1991) or Spencer (1991). Be warned, however, that some linguists use the term 'morpheme' in a concrete sense (so that e.g. *foxes* and *oxen* display different plural suffix morphemes) while others use it in a more abstract sense (whereby *foxes* and *oxen* both contain the morpheme 'plural', realised by distinct allomorphs -es and -en). Whenever you encounter these terms, make sure you know in which sense they are being used. My own preference is for the concrete sense; but I also try to avoid occasions for possible misunderstanding by using instead of 'morpheme' the terms 'affix', 'suffix' and 'root', as appropriate, wherever possible.

4 A word and its forms: inflection

4.1 Words and grammar: lexemes, word forms and grammatical words

In Chapter 1 I introduced the idea that some complex words have meanings that are so predictable that they do not have to be listed in a dictionary. Such words illustrate the fact that a word need not be a lexical item (while, conversely, idioms illustrate the fact that a lexical item need not be a word). However, I did not discuss the different varieties of non-lexical-item words. In this chapter we will focus on one variety: words that do not have to be listed because they are merely grammatically conditioned variants of a word that is more basic, in some sense – and which itself may or may not be listed, depending on whether its meaning is predictable or not.

By way of illustrating the notions 'more basic' and 'grammatically conditioned variant', let us consider the words *performs*, *performed* and *performance* in (1)–(3):

(1) This pianist performs in the local hall every week.
(2) Mary told us that this pianist performed in the local hall every week.
(3) The performance last week was particularly impressive.

All these words contain a suffix: *perform-s*, *perform-ed*, and *perform-ance*. However, the suffixes *-s* and *-ed* are dependent on the grammatical context in a way that the suffix *-ance* is not.

In (1), the reason why the verb *perform* has an *-s* suffix is that the subject of the verb (the noun phrase denoting the person doing the performing) is singular (*this pianist*), not plural (*these pianists*). (For more on grammatical terms such as 'subject', you may consult the syntax volume in the ETOTEL series.) It is easy for a native speaker to check that (4) and (5) 'feel wrong':

(4) *This pianist perform in the local hall every week.
(5) *These pianists performs in the local hall every week.

28

(You are reminded that the asterisk indicates that a sentence is unacceptable for some reason to do with grammar or with the structure of the language generally, rather than for reasons such as truthfulness or politeness.) Examples (4) and (5) are unacceptable because they violate a grammatical rule of English concerning 'agreement' between a verb and its subject: the -s suffix on the verb is obligatory when the subject is a singular noun phrase (that is, one for which *he*, *she* or *it* could be substituted), and forbidden when the subject is a plural noun phrase (one for which *they* could be substituted). The -s on the verb in (1) does not make any independent contribution to the meaning of the sentence, one might say; it simply reflects the fact that the subject of the sentence is singular rather than plural.

In (2), the aspect of the grammatical context that is relevant to the suffix -ed on *performed* is the fact that the verb *told* is in the past tense (that is, it refers to a past event, namely an earlier conversation with Mary). Mary's actual words in this earlier conversation were probably 'This pianist performs ...', not 'This pianist performed ...'. Why then is the word *performs* replaced by *performed* in the report of her words at (2)? The answer is that English grammar incorporates a rule about what is called 'sequence of tenses': if a verb of saying or thinking is in the past tense (as *told* is here), then a verb in any sentence reported as having been said or thought is likely to be shifted backwards in tense, so to speak: *performs* is replaced by *performed*, *performed* in turn is replaced by *had performed*, and *will perform* is replaced by *would perform*. Again, the -ed on *performed* does not make any independent contribution to the meaning of the sentence – for example, it does not (as one might expect) indicate that the series of concerts has ceased since the conversation with Mary took place. Instead, it is merely a grammatical consequence of the fact that the verb of saying is in the past tense (*told*) rather than the present (*tells*).

In (3), on the other hand, there is no grammatical factor that requires the presence of -ance on *performance*. The most one can say is that, in the context where *performance* occurs, one expects to find a noun rather than a verb such as *perform*, as illustrated by the unacceptability of (6):

(6) *The perform last week was particularly impressive.

However, there is nothing in this context that forces us to choose the noun *performance* in particular, or even another noun with the suffix -ance. Any noun (or at least any noun with an appropriate meaning) will do, as in:

(7) The performer last week was particularly impressive.
(8) The concert last week was particularly impressive.

We can describe the difference between *performance* on the one hand and *performs* and *performed* on the other by saying that the latter pair are grammatically conditioned variant forms of the verb *perform*, whereas *performance* is not a variant form of the verb, but rather a noun derived from it. We have encountered here another important distinction: between **derivational morphology** (the topic of Chapter 5), and so-called **inflectional morphology** or inflection (the topic of this chapter), which deals with the inflected forms of words, that is the kind of variation that words exhibit on the basis of their grammatical context. In Sections 4.2–5 we will look in more detail at inflection in English, while Sections 4.6 and 4.7 are concerned with kinds of inflection that require lexical listing because of unpredictability not of meaning but of shape.

It is necessary first, however, to introduce some terms that are more precise than the ordinary term 'word', which I have relied on heavily up to now. I have called *performs* and *performed* 'grammatically conditioned variants' or 'inflected forms' of 'the verb *perform*'. But if one compares (1) with (9), alongside the unacceptable examples (4) and (5), one can see that *perform* itself deserves to be called a grammatically conditioned variant too:

(9) These pianists perform in the local hall every week.

The fact that the verb appears with no suffix in (9), where the subject *these pianists* is plural, is just as much a matter of grammar as the fact that the verb appears with -*s* in (1), where the subject is singular. But it is awkward and confusing to describe *perform* in (9) as a form of itself! We need a new term for the more abstract kind of word of which the word forms *performs*, *performed* and *perform* are all inflectional variants. Let us call this more abstract kind of word a **lexeme**. Let us also introduce the convention that, where the distinction is important, words as lexemes are written in small capitals, while words as inflected forms continue to be represented in italics. We can now say that *performs*, *performed* and *perform* are all inflected forms of the lexeme PERFORM, and we can describe the grammatical function of *performed* by calling it the past tense form of the verb PERFORM. Equally, *told* in (2) is the past tense form of the verb TELL, and *pianists* in (9) is the plural form of the lexeme PIANIST.

Being abstract in this sense, a lexeme is not strictly speaking something that can be uttered or pronounced; only the word forms that belong to it can be. (For that reason, one could just as well use PERFORMS or PERFORMED as the label for the lexeme PERFORM; but, by convention, we refer to lexemes in English by means of their bare, unaffixed forms.) The most straightforward way to define the term **word form** is to tie it so closely to pronunciation that pronunciation is its sole criterion: two word forms are the same if and only if they are pronounced the same, or are homophonous. (Let us not be sidetracked by the fact that two words can be pronounced the same but spelled differently in English, and vice versa; in most domains of linguistic research, spoken language is more important than written.) It follows that the same word form can belong to two quite different lexemes, as does *rows* in (10) and (11):

(10) There were four rows of seats.

(11) One person rows the boat.

In (10), *rows* is the plural of the noun ROW meaning 'line of people or things', while in (11) it is one of the present tense forms of the verb ROW meaning 'propel with oars' (more precisely, it is the form used with subjects that can be replaced by *he*, *she* or *it*: so-called 'third person singular' subjects). Let us use the term **grammatical word** for designations like 'the plural of the noun ROW', 'the third person singular present tense of the verb ROW', and 'the past tense of the verb PERFORM . It will be seen that one lexeme may be represented by more than one word form, and one word form may represent more than one lexeme; what links a word form with a lexeme in a given context is the grammatical word that the word form expresses there. This may seem complicated at first, but as we discuss English inflection in more detail you will (I hope) come to appreciate the usefulness of these distinctions.

4.2 Regular and irregular inflection

At the beginning of this chapter, I introduced the topic of inflection by way of the distinction drawn in Chapter 2 between words that have to be listed in a dictionary and words that do not. I said that one does not have to list *performs* and *performed* alongside *perform*, or *pianists* alongside *pianist*, because they are merely grammatically conditioned variants of one basic word – of one lexeme, in fact. But it is not correct to say that dictionaries never have anything to say about inflectional morphology. This is because there are two reasons why a word form such as *pianists* does not have to be listed, and these reasons are independent. The first is that, once we know that an English word is a noun denoting a kind of thing that can be counted (if the noun is PIANIST or CAT, perhaps, but not ASTONISHMENT or RICE), then we can be confident that it will have a plural form with no idiosyncrasies of meaning: it will mean simply 'more than one X', whatever X may be. The second reason is that, unless otherwise specified, we can be confident that the plural form of any countable noun will be formed by adding to the singular form the suffix -*s* (or rather, the appropriate allomorph of this suffix); in other words, suffixing -*s* is the **regular** method of forming plurals.

That qualification 'unless otherwise specified' is crucial, however. Any native speaker of English, after a moment's thought, should be able to think of at least two or three nouns that form their plural in some other way than by adding -*s*: for example, CHILD has the plural form *children*, TOOTH has the plural *teeth*, and MAN has the plural *men*. The complete list of such nouns in English is not long, but it includes some that are extremely common. What this means for the dictionary entries for CHILD, TOOTH, MAN and the others is that, although nothing has to be said either about the fact that these nouns possess a plural form or about what it means, something does have to be said about how the plural is formed. Thus, for example, a dictionary entry for TOOTH will look like this:

> **tooth** *noun* (*plural* **teeth**). One of a set of hard white structures set in the jaw and used for biting and chewing.

Such nouns, in short, are **irregular** in their plural formation, and irregularity is a kind of idiosyncrasy that dictionaries need to acknowledge by indications such as '(*plural* **teeth**)' here. One can easily visualise a variety of English with no irregularity, but this would be unlike any variety actually in use. Readers of George Orwell's novel *Nineteen Eighty-Four* will recall that, in the politically purged variety of English called Newspeak, Orwell envisages the eradication of morphological irregularity along with opportunities for 'thoughtcrime', so that the plural of MAN in Newspeak is not *men* but *mans*. In reality as opposed to fiction, this sort of regularisation is a well-known feature of the speech of young children and of non-native learners. The very fact that regularisation takes place confirms that there is something about the irregular forms that requires them to be specially learned.

For English nouns, there is no difficulty in determining which is the regular method for forming the plural. However, the very fact that there is more than one method raises a potentially tricky question about morphemes and their allomorphs. Recall from Chapter 3 that the allomorphs of a morpheme may be distributed in a fashion that requires reference to individual lexical items, and also that allomorphs may differ from each other phonologically in idiosyncratic ways (as -*duce* differs from -*duct*-, and -*sume* from -*sump*-). If all this does not inhibit us from recognising them as allomorphs of one morpheme, what about the different plural suffixes exhibited by nouns such as *pianists, oxen, formulae* and *cacti* (these last three corresponding to the singular forms *ox, formula* and *cactus*)? Can we not classify -*s*, -*en*, -*ae* and -*i* as all allomorphs of a single 'plural' morpheme? Should we not also recognise a further allomorph that we might call 'vowel change', to accommodate *men* and *teeth*, which lack a suffix? Admittedly, these allomorphs are quite unlike each other in pronunciation – but if allomorphs are allowed to be differ somewhat, why cannot we allow them to be differ considerably? At what point, if any, does phonological divergence become too great?

This is a difficult question. Discussing it adequately would take us beyond the bounds of an elementary textbook on English word-structure. I mention it here in order to alert readers to be careful, when reading any text in which the term 'morpheme' is used, to make sure they understand how the author is using it: whether in a more concrete sense, oriented towards pronunciation (in terms of which -*s*, -*en*, -*ae* and -*i* represent different morphemes), or a more abstract sense, oriented towards meaning or grammatical function (in terms of which -*s*, -*en*, -*ae* and -*i* are all allomorphs of one morpheme). A good way to avoid any confusion is to use terms such as 'root', 'suffix' and 'prefix', wherever possible, rather than 'morpheme'. This is because, although there may be disagreement about whether to treat these plural suffixes as allomorphs of one morpheme, everyone agrees that they are distinct suffixes.

This question about suffixes with the same grammatical function has a bearing also on allomorphy affecting roots, such as *wife* and *wive-*. The phonological similarity between *wife* and *wive-*, and the fact that parallel alternations can be found (e.g. *knife* and *knive-*, *path* and *path-*, *house* and *house-*, in all of which a voiceless fricative consonant in the singular alternates with its voiced counterpart in the plural) are solid grounds for calling them allomorphs of one morpheme, as we saw in Chapter 3. In terms of Section 4.1, we clearly want to recognise *wife* and *wives* as expressing the singular and plural respectively of one lexeme WIFE. But does it follow that all the word forms of a lexeme must always share the same root morpheme? Does it ever happen that two word forms that behave grammatically like forms of one lexeme look so dissimilar that they seem to have no root morpheme in common (at least if 'morpheme' is given its more concrete sense)?

The answer is yes, but seldom (at least in English). Consider the lexeme GO. Because it is a verb, we expect it to have a past tense form, and this expectation is not disappointed. Surprisingly, however, what functions as the past tense form, namely *went*, is phonologically quite dissimilar to the verb's other forms *go*, *goes*, *going* and *gone*. Should we say, then, that *go* and *went* are allomorphs of one morpheme? Most linguists would say no; rather, they would treat this as showing that one lexeme may be represented by two (or more) quite distinct root morphemes (not allomorphs). The term given to this phenomenon is **suppletion**; *go* and *went* are said to be distinct roots (and hence distinct morphemes), standing in a suppletive relationship as representatives, in different grammatical contexts, of one lexeme. This view of suppletion, as a relationship between roots rather than between allomorphs, is consistent with the 'concrete' view of allomorphy outlined just now in relation to the plural suffixes.

From the point of view of allomorphy, it may seem that *go* and *went-* stand in just the same relationship as the plural suffixes *-s, -en, -ae* and *-i*; hence, if the term 'suppletion' is used for the former relationship, it should be used for the latter too. In fact, however, 'suppletion' is generally applied only to roots, not to affixes. This is because suppletion is generally seen as a relationship between forms of the same lexeme, whereas allomorphy need not be. For example, the allomorphs *wife* and *wive-* show up in forms of the lexeme WIFE, but the plural allomorphs [s], [z] and [ɪz] do not belong to any one lexeme – rather, they intersect with noun lexemes in such a way that any one regular noun chooses just one of these allomorphs, on the basis of the phonological criteria discussed in Chapter 3.

The discussion so far in this chapter has been rather general. In the remaining sections I will put flesh on the bones by discussing in more detail how inflection works in English, i.e. what grammatical words are associated with inflected lexemes, how these grammatical words are regularly expressed, and what kinds of irregularity they may display. Because the role of inflectional morphology in English is much smaller than in languages such as German or Russian (although greater than in Chinese), what needs to be said about each wordclass is relatively circumscribed. However, these sections will provide opportunities to illustrate a few further general issues and notions as well.

4.3 Forms of nouns

Most countable nouns in English have two word forms: a singular and a plural. Inflectionally, for any noun lexeme X, there are just two grammatical words, 'singular of X' and 'plural of X', contrasting in **number**. Thus, to the lexeme CAT there corresponds a singular form *cat*, consisting of just one morpheme, and a plural form *cats*, consisting of a root *cat* and the suffix *-s*. This suffix and its allomorphs were discussed in the previous chapter, and in this chapter we have noted that *-s* is the regular suffix for forming plurals. Irregular suffixes expressing plurality include *-i, -ae* and *-a* (as in *cacti, formulae, phenomena*) found with some relatively learned words borrowed from Latin or Greek; the suffix *-(r)en* that shows up only in *oxen, children* and *brethren*; and a very few others such as the Hebrew *-im* in *cherubim* and *kibbutzim*. (These borrowings from Latin and elsewhere are discussed further in Chapter 9.)

There are also some countable nouns that express their plural with no suffix at all. I have already mentioned two (*teeth*, *men*) where there is a change in the vowel of the root – or, more precisely, an allomorph of the root with a different vowel from the singular. However, there are also some whose plurals display not even a vowel change: for example, *sheep, fish, deer, trout*. An obvious question, therefore, is: if the plural and singular forms of these nouns are the same, how can we tell whether they are singular or plural? The answer is: according to the syntactic context. Consider the following examples:

(12) A deer was visible through the trees.
(13) Two deer were visible through the trees.

In (12) we can tell that *deer* is singular (more strictly, it represents the grammatical word 'singular of the lexeme DEER') because it is accompanied by the indefinite article *a*, which only ever accompanies singular nouns (e.g. *a cat*, not **a cats*), and because the form of BE found in (12), agreeing in singular number with the subject *a deer*, is *was*, not *were*. In (13), for parallel reasons, we can tell that *deer* is plural: the numeral *two* accompanies only plural nouns (*two cats*, not **two cat*), and the form of BE in (13) is the plural *were*.

The class of nouns which are unchanged in the plural (sometimes called 'zero-plural' nouns, if they are analysed as carrying a 'zero suffix') could conceivably be just as random as the class of those with vowel change (*tooth, man*, etc.) But in fact there seems to be a common semantic factor among the zero-plurals: they all denote animals, birds or fish that are either domesticated (SHEEP) or hunted (DEER), usually for food (TROUT, COD, PHEASANT). It is true that the relationship is not hard-and-fast: there are plenty of domesticated and game animals which have regular -*s* plurals (e.g. COW, GOAT, PIGEON, HEN). Nevertheless, the correlation is sufficiently close to justify regarding zero-plurals as in some degree regular, obeying a minority pattern of plural formation that competes with the dominant pattern of -*s*-suffixation.

In Section 4.2 I made the point that only some nouns have plural forms, namely nouns that refer to entities that are countable. That is why the forms *cats* and *pianists* exist, but not **astonishments* or **rices* – except perhaps in contexts where they can be interpreted as denoting countable entities, such as astonishing events or varieties of rice. But does that mean that all nouns referring to countable entities have both singular and plural forms? Not quite. There are a few nouns such as SCISSORS and PANTS which exist only in an -*s*-plural form, and which appear only in plural syntactic contexts, even though they denote single countable entities, as is shown by the contrast between (14) and (15):

(14) a. Those scissors belong in the top drawer.
     b. Your pants have a hole in the seat.
(15) a. *That scissors belongs in the top drawer.
     b. *Your pants has a hole in the seat.

This idiosyncratic lack of a morphological singular form (except in compounds such as *scissor factory*) creates a problem in contexts where the syntax seems to require such a form, as when the noun is preceded by the indefinite article *a* or *an*. We can say neither *a scissor* nor *a scissors*, and likewise neither *a pant* nor *a pants*. However, for these lexemes, there is a conventional circumlocution or **periphrastic form**: *pair of pants* and *pair of scissors* (as in *That pair of scissors belongs in the top drawer*).

The unusual nouns SCISSORS and PANTS provide an opportunity to deal with a possible doubt concerning whether the singular–plural contrast in nouns really deserves to be called inflectional. If inflection is a matter of grammatically conditioned variation, as I said in Section 4.1, it is easy to agree that (say) the contrast between *performs* in (1) (*This pianist performs ...*) and *perform* in (9) (*These pianists perform ...*) is inflectional, because it is a contrast imposed by the grammatical context (whether the subject noun phrase is singular or plural). But what about the noun phrases themselves? The choice between singular and plural there is determined not by grammar but by meaning, one may think – by what the speaker wants to say. If so, does this contrast really deserve to be called grammatically conditioned?

Despite the freedom to choose between, say, *this pianist* and *these pianists* as subjects of (9), there is still a sense in which English grammar affects the choice between singular and plural. It does so in the sense that it imposes the choice. In talking about a series of weekly piano concerts, we are free to be vague about the number of pianists who perform – except that we are forced by English grammar to be precise about whether there is one (*that pianist*) or more than one (*these pianists*). Like-wise, if I see a cat or some cats in the garden, I cannot report what I have seen without making it clear whether there was just one cat, as in (16) or more than one cat, as in (17). A formulation that is deliberately vague on that issue, such as (18), is unacceptable:

(16) I saw a cat in the garden.
(17) I saw (some) cats in the garden.
(18) *I saw cat in the garden.

The best we can do to express the intended content of (18) is use a circumlocution like *one or more cats* or *at least one cat*. In this respect,

English grammar contrasts with that of, for example, Chinese, where the singular–plural contrast is not expressed morphologically in nouns or verbs, and indeed is scarcely grammatically relevant at all. That does not mean that one cannot distinguish between one object and several when talking Chinese; it is just that the distinction is not imposed by Chinese grammar, which permits ambivalence about plurality. Curiously, the only nouns with which Chinese-style ambivalence is permissible in English are the unusual plural-only ones such as SCISSORS. Compare the meaning of (14a) with that of (19) and (20):

(19)   That pair of scissors belongs in the top drawer.
(20)   Those pairs of scissors belong in the top drawer.

(19) and (20) make it plain whether one or more than one pair of scissors is being talked about. On the other hand, (14a) is vague in just the way that (17) was meant to be; it can be interpreted as synonymous with either (19) or (20).

The singular–plural distinction is the only grammatical distinction that is expressed morphologically in English nouns. Some readers (especially those that know something of languages such as German or Latin) may be surprised that I have said nothing about the 'apostrophe-s' form: *pianist's, man's, child's, children's* etc. – do these not count as further inflected forms of the lexemes PIANIST, MAN and CHILD, namely 'possessive' forms? However, it is easy to show that what -'s attaches itself to is not a morphological unit such as noun root (e.g. *man*) but a syntactic unit, namely a noun phrase:

(21)   that man's bicycle
(22)   that old man's bicycle
(23)   that man next door's bicycle
(24)   that man you met yesterday's bicycle
(25)   that man you met's bicycle

Examples (21), (22) and (23) may seem compatible with saying that -'s is an affix that attaches to nouns, but (23) should give us pause (after all, it is the man, not the door, that owns the bicycle!), and (24) and (25) show conclusively that what -'s attaches to is a whole noun phrase (*that man you met (yesterday)*), including whatever modifiers it may contain following the noun at its head (*man*, in this instance). So -'s belongs in the study of syntax, not morphology. Its only morphological peculiarity is that, when the word immediately before it is a noun with the plural suffix -s, the two fuse, both in pronunciation and spelling, written -s': e.g. *these pianists' performances*, not *these pianists's performances*.

4.4 Forms of pronouns and determiners

In morphology we are mainly concerned with the behaviour of words which belong to **open classes**, namely nouns, adjectives, verbs and adverbs. These classes are so called because their membership can be added to, and indeed is added to constantly as new words come into use. By contrast, one does not expect in English to encounter a new pronoun (a word such as *I* or *she* or *us*) or a new preposition (a word such as *in* or *at* or *without*). However, determiners deserve a mention here because some of them, like nouns, display a singular–plural contrast, and pronouns combine a singular–plural contrast with contrast unique to them, between subject and non-subject forms.

We have already encountered the distinction between *this* and *these*, as in *this pianist* and *these pianists*. These are the singular and plural forms of the determiner lexeme THIS. Other determiners include THE, A(N) and SOME, but only one other determiner exhibits a singular–plural contrast: THAT, with singular and plural forms *that* and *those*. The determiners THAT and THIS demonstrate that number contrasts can have a grammatical effect inside noun phrase as well as between subject noun phrases and their accompanying verbs.

In many languages, the distinction that English expresses by word order in *John loves Mary* and *Mary loves John* is expressed by inflectional means on the words corresponding to *Mary* and *John*. In English, the same technique is used for one small closed class of lexemes, namely personal pronouns. If one replaces *John* and *Mary* with the appropriate pronouns in these two examples, the outcome is as in (26) and (27):

(26) He loves her.
(27) She loves him.

He and *him* are sometimes said to contrast in **case**, *he* belonging to the **nominative case** and *him* belonging to the **accusative case**. This kind of inflection has only a marginal role in English, being limited to pronouns; but, if we treat (say) HE as a lexeme, we must recognise it as having two forms: *he* and *him*. It is striking that the relationship between nominative and accusative forms is consistently suppletive, as in *I/me, she/her, we/us,* and *they/them*, except that for YOU the two forms are identical (*you*). This is consistent with the fact that pronouns are very common, and suppletion affects only very common words such as GO.

If *he* and *him* are forms of the lexeme HE, and *we* and *us* are forms of WE (and so on), what are we to say about corresponding words with a possessive meaning: *his* and *our*, as well as *my, her, your* and *their*? Syntactically and semantically, these words fulfil just the same role as noun phrases with the aspostrophe-s discussed in the previous section: *his bicycle* means 'the bicycle belonging to him' just as *that man's bicycle* means 'the bicycle belonging to that man'. One possibility is to say that these are pronoun forms belonging to a third case, the genitive or possessive, which stand in for apostrophe-s forms in noun phrases that consist only of a personal pronoun. Another is to classify these words as determiners, because they perform a determiner-like role and cannot be combined with other determiners (we cannot say *the my hat* any more than we can say *the that hat*). But these are issues of syntax rather than morphology. For present purposes, we need merely note how *his*, *our* and the rest behave, while leaving their exact grammatical classification undecided.

4.5 Forms of verbs

We have already discussed some forms of English verbs in Sections 4.1 and 4.2, such as *performs, performed* and *perform*. In English, a verb lexeme has at most five distinct forms, as illustrated here with GIVE:

(28) GIVE
    a. third person singular present tense: *gives*
      e.g. *Mary gives a lecture every year.*
    b. past tense: *gave*
      e.g. *Mary gave a lecture last week.*
    c. progressive participle: *giving*
      e.g. *Mary is giving a lecture today.*
    d. perfect or passive participle: *given*
      e.g. *Mary has given a lecture today.*
      The lecture is always given by Mary.
    e. basic form (used everywhere else):   *give*
      e.g. *Mary may give a lecture.*
      Mary wants to give a lecture.
      Mary and John give a lecture every year.

The contrast between present at (28a) and past at (28b) is a contrast of **tense**. The other dimensions of contrast manifested in (28a) are **person** (third person versus the rest) and **number** (singular versus plural, just as for nouns and pronouns). However, because only one word form (*gives*) exhibits these contrasts, they play a much smaller inflectional role in modern English verbs than in Old English verbs, as we shall see in Chapter 9.

For the form labelled 'perfect or passive participle', two examples are given, because perfect and passive contexts can be distinguished clearly; however, it is a peculiarity of English verb morphology that the corresponding forms are always the same. Another way of putting this is that, for any verb V, the grammatical words 'perfect participle of V' and 'passive participle of V' are expressed by the same word form.

I said that a verb lexeme has at most five forms. In fact, most verbs have only four forms, because the past tense and the perfect (or passive) participle forms are the same. This is true for all regular verbs (those that form the past tense with the suffix -ed), such as PERFORM (which I used for illustration in Section 4.1):

(29) PERFORM
    a. third person singular present tense: *performs*
    b. past tense: *performed*
    c. progressive participle: *performing*
    d. perfect or passive participle: *performed*
    e. basic form (used everywhere else):   *perform*

When two grammatical words that are distinct for some lexemes are systematically identical for others, as here, these forms are said to be syncretised, or to exhibit **syncretism**. The same syncretism also occurs with some irregular verbs, such as DIG and STING (past = perfect participle *dug, stung*) and all those that use the suffix -*t*, such as BEND, FEEL, and TEACH (*bent, felt, taught*). In all, 150 or so verbs are irregular in that they do not use the -*ed* suffix. I will not list them all here, however, because the study of these irregularities belongs to grammar rather than to word-formation.

Other verbs or verb-like words whose behaviour belongs to grammar rather than to word-formation are the auxiliaries, such as BE and HAVE, and modals, such as CAN, MUST, MAY. But they deserve mention here because their various forms distinguish an unusually small or large range of grammatical words. Instead of the usual verbal maximum of five forms, modals distinguish only two (e.g. *can, could*) or even just one (e.g. *must*), while BE distinguishes eight (*am, is, are, was, were, being, been, be*).

4.6 Forms of adjectives

Many English adjectives exhibit three forms, for example GREEN here:

(30) Grass is green.
(31) The grass is greener now than in winter.
(32) The grass is greenest in early summer.

The grammatical words that *green, greener* and *greenest* express are the positive, comparative and superlative of GREEN, contrasting on the dimension of **comparison**. Other adjectives with similar forms are:

(33) *Positive*   *Comparative*   *Superlative*
      happy   happier   happiest
      long   longer   longest
      pure   purer   purest
      untidy   untidier   untidiest
      good   better   best

All these exhibit a regular pattern of suffixation with -er and -est, except for *better* and *best*, which are suppletive.

The justification for saying that comparative and superlative forms of adjectives belong to inflectional rather than to derivational morphology is that there are some grammatical contexts in which comparative or superlative adjectives are unavoidable, anything else (even if semantically appropriate) being ill-formed:

(34) a. This field is greener than that one.
      b. *This field is green than that one.
      c. *This field is fertile than that one.
(35) a. The greenest fields of all are here.
      b. *The green fields of all are here.
      c. *The superior fields of all are here.

On the basis of our experience with plurals of countable nouns and past tense forms of verbs, then, you will probably expect that every adjective lexeme should possess a comparative and a superlative form (or, at any rate, every adjective denoting a property that can be present to a greater or lesser degree). However, it is striking that many adjectives lack these forms:

(36) *Curiouser and curiouser!
(37) *This field is fertiler than that one.
(38) *The fertilest fields of all are here.

(You may recognise (36) from Lewis Carrol's *Alice's Adventures in Wonderland* as something that Alice scolds herself for saying.) But it is not that the content of (36)–(38) is inexpressible in English; rather, instead of the suffixes -er and -est, we use periphrastic forms with *more* or *most*:

(39) More and more curious!
(40) This field is more fertile than that one.
(41) The most fertile fields of all are here.

Broadly speaking, the suffixes -er and -est appear on adjectives whose basic form has one syllable, or two provided that the second syllable ends in a vowel (e.g. *tidy*, *yellow*), while longer adjectives usually require the periphrasis.

4.7 Conclusion and summary

Some words (lexemes) have more than one word form, depending on the grammatical context or on choices that grammar forces us to make (for example, in nouns, between singular and plural). This kind of word-formation is called 'inflectional'. In so far as grammar affects all words alike, the existence of inflected word forms does not have to be noted in the dictionary; however, the word forms themselves must be listed if they are irregular.

Inflection affects nouns, verbs, adjectives and a few adverbs, as well as the closed classes of pronouns, determiners, auxiliaries and modals. However, the maximum number of distinct inflected forms for any open-class lexeme is small:

nouns:	2	e.g. *cat, cats*
verbs:	5	e.g. *gives, gave, giving, given, give*
adjectives:	3	e.g. *green, greener, greenest*
adverbs:	3	e.g. *soon, sooner, soonest*

Inflection thus plays a much more modest role in modern English than in German (for example), or in Old English (as we shall see in Chapter 9). In some languages, a lexeme may have hundreds or even thousands of distinct forms. On the other hand, English makes more use of inflection than languages such as Afrikaans, Vietnamese and Chinese, which have little or none. Why languages should differ so enormously in this respect is a fascinating question, but one that we cannot delve into here.

Exercises

1. In each of the following groups of word forms, identify those that are (or can be, according to context) forms of the same lexeme:

    (a) woman, woman's, women, womanly, girl
    (b) greenish, greener, green, greens
    (c) written, wrote, writer, rewrites, writing.

2. What word form represents each of the following grammatical words?

    (a) the plural of the noun NOOSE
    (b) the plural of the noun GOOSE
    (c) the plural of the noun MOOSE
    (d) the past tense of the verb PLAY
    (e) the past tense of the verb LAY
    (f) the past tense of the verb LIE 'rest horizontally'

(g)   the past tense of the verb LIE 'tell untruths'
(h)   the third person singular past of the verb BE
(i)   the perfect participle of the verb DIVE
(j)   the perfect participle of the verb STRIVE
(k)   the perfect participle of the verb GLIDE
(l)   the perfect participle of the verb RIDE
(m) the perfect participle of the verb STRIDE
(n)   the accusative of the pronoun YOU
(o)   the accusative of the pronoun WE

3. Which of the forms in question 2 are irregular? Are any of them suppletive?

4. Identify at least one adjective, not mentioned in the chapter, that has a suppletive comparative form.

5. In the chapter, it was said that, broadly speaking, the superlative suffix -est is limited to single-syllable adjectives. Some of the following adjectives show that this is an oversimplification. Which ones? (Consult a native speaker, if necessary. Do not be surprised if different speakers disagree!)

GENTLE   COMMON   PRECISE   REMOTE

Recommendations for reading

My use of the terms 'lexeme', 'word form' and 'grammatical word' is heavily influenced by Matthews (1991). For a readable and engaging discussion of the distinction between regular and irregular inflection, and of its wide implications for our understanding of how language is processed in the brain, see Pinker (1999).

Aronoff (1994) discusses the fact that the same word form serves as both perfect participle and passive participle in English, despite the fact that syntactically the two are quite distinct. Citing similar examples, he points out the wider implications of this phenomenon for morphological theory.

5 A word and its relatives: derivation

5.1 Relationships between lexemes

In Section 4.1 we discussed the words *perform, performs, performed* and *performance*. I argued that *perform, performs* and *performed* were grammatically conditioned variants of one lexeme PERFORM, but *performance* was not one of these variants. The reason was that, whereas there are grammatical factors that determine the choice between *perform, performs* and *performed* (in appropriate contexts), there is no grammatical factor that requires specifically the presence of *-ance* on *performance*. To put it another way: there are contexts where, if any verb appears, it must carry the third person singular suffix *-s*, but there are no contexts where, if a noun appears, it must carry the suffix *-ance*. The suffix *-ance* is not one of the small class of suffixes (so-called 'inflectional' suffixes) whose use is tightly determined by grammar. What sort of suffix is it, then? A short answer is that, not being inflectional, it must be **derivational**, since the term 'derivation' is used for all aspects of word-structure involving affixation that is not inflectional. The purpose of this chapter is to put flesh on the bones of this purely negative definition, showing something of how derivation works in English.

Since *performance* is not a variant of the lexeme PERFORM, it must belong to some other lexeme, which may itself have more than one form. What lexeme could this be? This question is easy to answer when we notice that, alongside *performance*, there is a plural form *performances*. Just as *cat* and *cats* are the two forms (singular and plural) of the lexeme CAT, it makes sense to regard *performance* and *performances* as the two forms of a lexeme PERFORMANCE. This tells us something about the relationship between *perform* and *performance*: it is a relationship not between word forms but rather between lexemes. (Strictly, then, in terms of our typographical convention, we should call it a relationship between PERFORM and PERFORMANCE.) Thus derivational morphology is concerned with one kind of relationship between lexemes.

There are many ways in which lexemes can be related. We are not concerned here with relationships solely of meaning (such as the synonymy of AUBERGINE and EGGPLANT) or of sound (such as the homonymy of ROW 'line of people or things' and ROW 'propel with oars'). Rather, we are concerned mainly with relationships involving affixation, and the grammatical and semantic tasks that such affixation can perform. As we will see, both the affixes and their tasks are quite diverse. An encyclopedic coverage of all the English derivational processes would be impossible in a book of this size, but I will attempt to supply a representative selection, so as to equip the reader to notice and to describe, with reasonable confidence, other processes not mentioned here.

I will introduce the term **base** for the partially complete word form to which an affix is attached so as to create either an inflected word form or a new lexeme. (Equivalently, the base for an affixation process is what remains if the affix is removed.) Some bases are roots, whether bound (e.g. *wive-*, the base for *wives*) or free (e.g. *cat*, the base for *cats*). Others, however, already contain a root and one or more affixes, such as *helpful* in its capacity as the base for *helpfulness*.

5.2 Word classes and conversion

Much of this chapter will be concerned with how adjectives can be derived from nouns, nouns from verbs, and so on. It is important therefore that terms for **word classes** such as 'adjective', 'noun' and 'verb' should be properly understood. (What I have just called word classes are the same as what in traditional terminology are called **parts of speech** and what many contemporary linguists call **lexical categories**.) Readers who are confident that they can recognise a noun or a verb when they see one may feel entitled to skip to the next section. On the other hand, I suspect that many such confident readers think that the word class to which a lexeme belongs is mainly determined by its meaning. That belief is incorrect. If you feel tempted by it, please do not skip this section!

In school, you may once have been told that verbs are 'doing words', while nouns are 'thing words' and adjectives 'describing words'. The trouble with these meaning-based definitions is that, if one takes them seriously, they require us to lump together lexemes whose grammatical behaviour is quite different, and distinguish between ones whose grammatical behaviour is similar. Consider again the lexeme PERFORM, which looks like a prototypical 'doing word', denoting something that actors and musicians do. The lexeme PERFORMANCE denotes the same activity, surely. Does that mean that PERFORM and PERFORMANCE belong to the same word class? That can hardly be right, since they occur in such different syntactic contexts, and since (in the terminology of Chapter 4) their inflectional behaviour is so different: PERFORMANCE has the two forms *performance* (singular) and *performances* (plural), while PERFORM has the four forms *performs, performed, performing* and *perform*. In fact, as we have seen, PERFORMANCE is a noun and PERFORM is a verb. This classification can be made as in Chapter 4, solely on the basis of their syntactic and inflectional behaviour, with no appeal to meaning – and indeed meaning may be positively misleading, since a performance is not obviously a 'thing'.

Compare now the lexemes PERFORM and RESEMBLE. Is the latter a 'doing word' too? That seems scarcely appropriate. Resembling, one may think, hardly counts as an activity. To say that (for example) my great-uncle William resembles a giraffe is not to report some action of his, but rather to describe him. Should we then lump RESEMBLE in with other supposed 'describing words' – adjectives such as TALL and INTERESTING? Again, this meaning-motivated conclusion falls foul of syntactic and inflectional evidence. These adjectives have comparative and superlative forms (*taller, tallest*) or phrasal substitutes for them (*more interesting, most interesting*); on the other hand, RESEMBLE has a set of forms (*resembles, resembled, resembling* and *resemble*) exactly parallel to the forms of PERFORM, and used in broadly parallel syntactic contexts. So to identify verbs as 'doing words' risks misleading us into neglect of the syntactic and inflectional parallels that justify classifying not only PERFORM but also RESEMBLE as a verb.

Does that mean, then, that a lexeme cannot have both noun forms (singular and plural) and verb forms (past, third person singular present, and so on)? If part of identifying a lexeme is identifying what word class it belongs to, then that must be true – but trivially so, because it amounts to decreeing that a root that can carry verbal suffixes such as *-ed* and *-ing* as well as the noun plural suffix *-s* must belong to two lexemes, not one. The more interesting question, then, is: do such roots exist? The answer is certainly yes. For example, HOPE and FEAR have both noun forms (*her hope/fear for the future*) and verb forms (*she hoped/feared that it would rain*). Other similarly ambivalent words are WISH, DESIRE, FATHER (a verb in *He fathered seven children*), and COOK. Does this mean that the concept 'word class', as I have used it, is too vague or inconsistent to be useful?

The answer is no, for two reasons. The first involves the proportion of our noun–verb vocabulary that is ambivalent in this way. Although numerous, it is still heavily outnumbered by the proportion that is either purely noun-like in its grammatical behaviour (e.g. DOOR, SISTER, DESK, JOY) or purely verb-like (e.g. HEAR, SPEAK, WRITE, BELIEVE). Admittedly, one can imagine a language in which a far higher proportion of the vocabulary is ambivalent in the way we are discussing, and in respect of such a language one might well argue that many or most lexemes did not belong to identifiable word classes. Such claims have in fact been made in relation to some languages in the Austronesian family, which contains (for example) Malay, Tagalog, and the languages of Polynesia, as well as some native languages of western Canada and the US Pacific coast. Even there, however, it seems generally necessary to distinguish nominal (i.e. 'nouny') and verbal syntactic structure, despite the fact that the class of lexemes that can occur in each type of structure is almost the same.

A second kind of reason has to do with English in particular. Let us compare HOPE and FEAR as verbs with other verbs that can be followed by *that*-clauses, as in (1):

(1) a. She stated that it would rain.
 b. She knew that it would rain.
 c. She denied that it would rain.
 d. She admitted that it would rain.
 e. She acknowledged that it would rain.

For all of these sentences we can identify a nominal counterpart, that is a counterpart of the form *her ... that it would rain*:

(2) a. her statement that it would rain
 b. her knowledge that it would rain
 c. her denial that it would rain
 d. her admission that it would rain
 e. her acknowledgement that it would rain

What is striking about the nouns in (2) is that they all involve a suffix added to the basic form of the verb in (1) (possibly with some other phonological change, as in *knowledge* and *admission*). There are few verb–noun pairs that one can use in the contexts of (1) and (2) such that the basic and suffixed forms are the other way round, the noun supplying the base and the verb being derived from it by means of a suffix. In morphological terms, therefore, it makes sense to say that the verbal construction in (1) is basic, the nominal construction in (2) being derived from it. But this has implications for HOPE and FEAR as well. If we look only at (3) and (4), we have no basis for deciding whether these lexemes are basically nominal or basically verbal:

(3) a. She hoped that it would rain.
 b. She feared that it would rain.
(4) a. her hope that it would rain
 b. her fear that it would rain

However, as soon as we notice that (3) and (4) are parallel to (1) and (2) respectively, we have a ground for concluding that HOPE and FEAR are basically verbal. The nominal contexts of (4) are parallel to those of (2), where the nouns are clearly derived from verbs; so it makes sense to say that the nouns HOPE and FEAR in (4) are derived from verbs too, even though they carry no affix.

The notion that derivation can occur without any overt change in shape may at first seem strange. Some linguists have accordingly decided that HOPE and FEAR, as nouns, are really 'zero-derived', carrying a phonologically empty and therefore unpronounceable 'zero suffix': HOPE-Ø, FEAR-Ø. Others have preferred to say that one of the processes available in derivational morphology is **conversion**, whereby a lexeme belonging to one class can simply be 'converted' to another, without any overt change in shape. We do not need to decide here which is the better style of analysis, though I will generally refer to the phenomenon as 'conversion'. Either way, these ambivalent words present the problem of determining which word class the basic form belongs to. Sometimes, as with HOPE and FEAR, a decisive argument involving parallels with affixed lexemes can be found. Sometimes, despite the risks already mentioned of relying on meaning as a criterion, the basic meaning seems clearly appropriate to one word class rather than another; for example, few would deny that, even though FATHER can function as a verb, it is the noun (as in *my father*) that is more basic. In respect of COOK, working out the direction of conversion is left as an exercise at the end of the chapter.

5.3 Adverbs derived from adjectives

In Chapter 2 I invited readers to think about the adjective DIOECIOUS, meaning 'having male and female flowers on different plants'. Certainly, DIOECIOUS must be listed in any reasonably complete dictionary of English. I argued, however, that the corresponding adverb DIOECIOUSLY would not have to be listed, because both its existence and its meaning can be taken for granted once the existence of DIOECIOUS is acknowledged. This neatly illustrates the distinction between lexemes and lexical items: DIOECIOUSLY is a distinct lexeme from DIOECIOUS, since it belongs to a different word class, but it is not a distinct lexical item. This also illustrates a widespread though not universal characteristic of derivational processes: unlike inflection, they can change the word class of the bases to which they apply.

Some introductory treatments of English grammar talk as if not just many but all adverbs end in *-ly*. If that were true, it would be an unusual word class, all of its members being derived. In fact, simple or mono-morphemic adverbs, though few in number, include some very common words (OFTEN, SELDOM, NEVER, SOON), and some other adverbs are mor-phologically complex without containing -*ly* (NOWHERE, EVERYWHERE, TODAY, YESTERDAY). Also, there are common adverbs that are formed by conversion: FAST (as in *The car was driven fast*) and HARD (as in *They worked hard*), derived from the adjective FAST (as in *a fast car*) and HARD (as in *hard work*).

5.4 Nouns derived from nouns

Not all derivational processes change word class. English has deriva-tional processes that yield nouns with meanings such as 'small X', 'female X', 'inhabitant of X', 'state of being an X' and 'devotee of or expert on X'. Here are some examples – though by no means a complete list, either of the affixes or of their possible meanings:

(5) 'small X': -*let*, -*ette*, -*ie*
e.g. *droplet, booklet, cigarette, doggie*
(6) 'female X': -*ess*, -*ine*
e.g. *waitress, princess, heroine*
(7) 'inhabitant of X': -*er*, -*(i)an*
e.g. *Londoner, New Yorker, Texan, Glaswegian*
(8) 'state of being an X': -*ship*, -*hood*
kingship, ladyship, motherhood, priesthood
(9) 'devotee of or expert on X': -*ist*, -*ian*
e.g. *contortionist, Marxist, logician, historian*

If you think about these, you should come to agree that all or nearly all of them must count as lexical items. Many of them have unpredictable meanings (a cigarette is not merely a small cigar, and a booklet is not merely a small book; BROTHERHOOD means not 'the state of being a brother' but rather 'secret or semi-secret society'). Also, the very exist-ence of some of these words seems arbitrary. Why is there a word ACTRESS (albeit less used now than formerly), but there has never been a word 'WRITRESS' to designate a woman writer? (I use quotation marks here to identify non-existent but plausible lexemes.) Why do we have DROPLET but not 'GRAINLET' or 'LUMPLET'? It is merely an accident that some of these words have come into general use while others have not, so those that do exist must be lexically listed. This 'gappiness' also helps to confirm (should confirmation be needed) that these affixes are deri-vational rather than inflectional, even though they do not change word class.

The examples GLASWEGIAN, LOGICIAN and HISTORIAN illustrate, at least superficially, the possibility that the base for a derivational process may be bound rather than free – a possibility already noted in Section 3.2, where bound roots were discussed. *Glaswegian* contains an idiosyncratic bound allomorph *Glasweg-* of the free morpheme *Glasgow*, which is also the only word form belonging to the lexeme GLASGOW. In *logician* and *historian*, the base allomorphs differ superficially from the free word forms *logic* and *history* in the position of main stressed syllable. However, this stress difference has many parallels (compare *Canada* and *Canadian*, *mathematics* and *mathematician*), and many linguists would argue that it is due to a phonological process. If so, then the base to which *-ian* is attached in *historian* (for example) can be regarded as the same as the free allomorph *history*.

5.5 Nouns derived from members of other word classes

Nouns derived from adjectives and from verbs are extremely numerous, and it should be easy for you to think of many other examples on the lines of those given here. Here are some suffixes used to derive nouns from adjectives:

(10) *-ity*, e.g. *purity, equality, ferocity, sensitivity*
(11) *-ness*, e.g. *goodness, tallness, fierceness, sensitiveness*
(12) *-ism*, e.g. *radicalism, conservatism*

All these three suffixes mean basically 'property of being X', where X is the base adjective. Of the three, *-ness* is the most widely applicable, and the great majority of nouns formed with it are not lexical items as defined in Chapter 2. For example, once one has learned DIOECIOUS, one can be confident of both the existence and the meaning of DIOECIOUS-NESS. Even so, at least one noun in *-ness* is lexicalised: HIGHNESS, which means not 'property of being high' (for which we use HEIGHT), but rather 'royal personage', as in *Her Royal Highness*.

Some of these nouns are formed from bases other than the free form of the corresponding adjective, e.g. FEROCITY from *feroc-* (not *ferocious*), CONSERVATISM from *conservat-* (not *conservative*). The FEROCITY pattern is fairly general for adjectives in *-ious* (compare RAPACITY, CAPACITY alongside *rapacious* and *capacious*) but not absolutely general (for example, to *delicious* and *specious* there correspond DELICIOUSNESS and SPECIOUSNESS, not 'DELICITY' or 'SPECITY'). This gappiness is a reason for counting all nouns in *-ity* as lexical items, and its implications will be discussed further in Chapter 8.

Even more numerous are suffixes for deriving nouns from verbs. Here are just a few:

(13)   *-ance, -ence*, e.g. *performance, ignorance, reference, convergence*
(14)   *-ment*, e.g. *announcement, commitment, development, engagement*
(15)   *-ing*, e.g. *painting, singing, building, ignoring*
(16)   *-((a)t)ion*, e.g. *denunciation, commission, organisation, confusion*
(17)   *-al*, e.g. *refusal, arrival, referral, committal*
(18)   *-er*, e.g. *painter, singer, organiser, grinder*

The suffixes in (13)–(17) all have much the same function (they form abstract nouns meaning 'activity or result of Xing'), but they are certainly not freely interchangeable: for example, we have PERFORMANCE but no 'PERFORMMENT' or 'PERFORMATION', and we have COMMITMENT, COMMITTAL and COMMISSION but no 'COMMITTANCE'. It is true that some verbs allow a choice of suffixes (e.g. COMMIT), but the nouns thus formed are not synonyms: one can commit a crime, commit an accused person for trial, or commit oneself to a task, but, of the three nouns, only COMMISSION corresponds to the first meaning, only COMMITTAL to the second, and only COMMITMENT to the third. Comparison of ANNOUNCE-MENT (corresponding to ANNOUNCE) and DENUNCIATION (corresponding to DENOUNCE) confirms that verbs that are similar in shape do not necessarily choose the same noun-forming suffixes (ANNUNCIATION scarcely exists outside the idiomatic context *the Annunciation of the Blessed Virgin*). Sometimes a noun's meaning may even be quite far removed from that of the corresponding verb: for example, IGNORE means 'deliberately refuse to acknowledge', yet IGNORANCE means not 'deliberate refusal to acknowledge' but rather 'unawareness'. Of the suffixes in (13)–(17), *-ing* is the most general, and indeed all verbs can form nouns with it irrespective of whatever other suffixes they may use; but even *-ing* nouns may have semantic and grammatical idiosyncrasies (one can look at a painting or a building, but one listens to a song rather than to a singing). This semantic waywardness will be discussed further in Chapter 8, along with a phonological restriction on the use of noun-forming *-al*.

The suffix *-er* in (18) is the one most generally used for forming nouns denoting a person performing the action of the corresponding verb (agent nouns). But it is not the only agent suffix (TYPIST and INFORMANT use other suffixes), and this is not its only function; for example, DIGGER is more likely to denote a piece of machinery than a person, and we have already encountered *-er* in Section 5.4 with the meaning 'inhabitant of' (e.g. LONDONER).

This is an appropriate place to recall that, although affixation is by far the most common way in which lexemes are derived in English, it is not the only way. Some non-affixal ways of deriving abstract nouns (other than conversion) are:

(19) change in the position of the stress, e.g. nouns PÉRMIT, TRÁNSFER alongside verbs PERMÍT, TRANSFÉR

(20) change in the final consonant, e.g. nouns BELIEF, PROOF, DEFENCE alongside verbs BELIEVE, PROVE, DEFEND

(21) change in a vowel, e.g. nouns SONG, SEAT alongside verbs SING, SIT.

By contrast with some languages, however, the derivational use that English makes of vowel change is minimal. Languages that exploit it much more consistently are members of the Semitic family, such as Arabic and Hebrew.

5.6 Adjectives derived from adjectives

In this category, prefixes predominate. The only suffix of note is -ish, meaning 'somewhat X', as in GREENISH, SMALLISH, REMOTISH 'rather remote'. By contrast, the prefix un- meaning 'not' is extremely widespread: for example, UNHAPPY, UNSURE, UNRELIABLE, UNDISCOVERED. Because it is so common, most dictionaries do not attempt to list all un- adjectives. This does not mean, however, that un- can be prefixed to all adjectives quite freely; we do not find, for example, 'UNGOOD' with the meaning 'bad' (though George Orwell included that word in the Newspeak vocabulary devised for *Nineteen Eighty-Four*).

Another negative prefix is in-, with allomorphs indicated by the variant spellings il-, ir- and im-, as in INTANGIBLE, ILLEGAL, IRRESPONSIBLE and IMPOSSIBLE. It is more restricted than un-, largely for historical reasons such as will be discussed in Chapter 9. For the present, it is worth noting the existence of pairs of more or less synonymous adjectives, one of which is negated with un- and the other with in- or one of its allomorphs:

(22) eatable/uneatable   edible/inedible
     readable/unreadable   legible/illegible
     lawful/unlawful   legal/illegal
     touchable/untouchable   tangible/intangible

Such examples confirm that the use of in- is lexically restricted. As the negative counterpart of EDIBLE, UNEDIBLE sounds possible, especially if the speaker has limited education and has not encountered, or has momentarily forgotten, the form INEDIBLE. However, 'INEATABLE' as the counterpart of EATABLE is not a form that any English speaker would spontaneously use.

5.7 Adjectives derived from members of other word classes

Some of the processes that derive adjectives from verbs straddle the divide between derivation and inflection in a way that we have not yet encountered. In Chapter 4, we met the suffixes *-ed*, *-en* and *-ing*, and vowel change, in passive and progressive participle forms of verbs. However, such forms (in italics in (23)) can also be adjectives:

(23) a. a not very *interesting* book
      b. The party-goers sounded very *drunk*.
      c. The car seemed more *damaged* than the lamp-post.

The modifier *very* and the comparative construction (*more ... than*) show that *interesting*, *drunk* and *damaged* are adjectives here, not forms of the verb lexemes INTEREST, DRINK and DAMAGE. (Notice that *very* cannot modify verbs, so one cannot say **That book very interested me.*) As for *drunk*, its status as belonging to a distinct lexeme here is confirmed by its special meaning ('intoxicated through drinking alcohol'), not predictable from the meaning of the verb DRINK ('swallow liquid').

Further suffixes that commonly form adjectives from verbs, with their basic meanings, are:

(24) *-able* 'able to be Xed': *breakable, readable, reliable, watchable*
(25) *-ent*, *-ant* 'tending to X': *repellent, expectant, conversant*
(26) *-ive* 'tending to X': *repulsive, explosive, speculative*

Expectations derived from these basic meanings can, as usual in derivation, be overridden; for example, CONVERSANT does not mean 'tending to converse'. We have already encountered *-able* in (22), where the variant, or allomorph, *-ible* is also illustrated. What is striking about the *-ible* words in (22) is that their bases, although they have clearly identifiable verbal meanings such as 'eat', 'read' and 'touch', are bound rather than free. Some of these bound verb roots appear in a number of derived lexemes, such as the *aud-* root that occurs in (IN)AUDIBLE, AUDITION, AUDIENCE and AUDITORY.

Suffixes that form adjectives from nouns are more numerous. Here are some:

(27) *-ful*, e.g. *joyful, hopeful, helpful, meaningful*
(28) *-less*, e.g. *joyless, hopeless, helpless, meaningless*
(29) *-al*, e.g. *original, normal, personal, national*
(30) *-ish*, e.g. *boyish, loutish, waspish, selfish*

As will be seen, adjectives in *-ful* and *-less* tend to come in pairs, although the correspondence is not exact: we have SLOTHFUL but not 'SLOTHLESS', and PENNILESS but not 'PENNIFUL'. This confirms again that, even when the meaning of a potential word may be easily guessable (a 'slothless' person would be hardworking, and a 'penniful' person would be well off), the existence of the word is not guaranteed.

5.8 Verbs derived from verbs

This section is unusual in that all the affixes that I will mention in it are prefixes. Most prominent are *re-* and the negative or 'reversive' prefixes *un-*, *de-* and *dis-*, as in the following examples:

(31) paint, enter   repaint, re-enter
(32) tie, tangle   untie, untangle
(33) compose, sensitise   decompose, desensitise
(34) entangle, believe   disentangle, disbelieve

The prefix *re-* has already figured in our discussion in Chapter 2 of the relationship between morphemes and meaning. Semantically, the examples in (31)–(34) are mostly straightforward, although those with *de-* are less so: to decompose is not to undo the creative work of a musical composer!

Also worth mentioning here is the relationship between the verbs in the left and right columns in (35):

(35) *Intransitive*   *Transitive*
      LIE (*past* lay)   LAY (*past* laid)
      RISE (*past* rose)   RAISE (*past* raised)
      FALL (*past* fell)   FELL (*past* felled)
      SIT (*past* sat)   SET (*past* set)

Transitive verbs (or verbs used transitively) are ones with an 'object' noun phrase, usually indicating the thing or person that is the goal of the action of the verb, as *the book* is the object of *laid* in (36a). **Intransitive** verbs, such as *lay* in (36b), lack such an object.

(36) a. Jill laid the book on the table.
      b. The book lay on the table.

The transitive verbs in (35) are all **causative**, that is they mean 'cause to X', where X stands for the meaning of the corresponding intransitive. Causative–incausative verb-pairs are common in English, but they nearly all involve conversion, as in (37), rather than either affixation or the kind of vowel change seen in (35):

(37) a. Jill boiled the water.
      b. The water boiled.

The examples in (35) represent a residue of a vowel-change pattern that was more widespread at an earlier stage of the language. More will be said about such historical developments in Chapter 9.

5.9 Verbs derived from members of other word classes

Verbs derived from nouns and from adjectives are numerous. Some affixes for deriving verbs from nouns are:

(38) *de-*, e.g. *debug, deforest, delouse*
(39) *-ise*, e.g. *organise, patronise, terrorise*
(40) *-(i)fy*, e.g. *beautify, gentrify, petrify*

There are also some common verbs that are derived by replacing the final voiceless consonant of a noun with a voiced one, perhaps with some vowel change too (parallel to the relationship between BELIEF and BELIEVE, although there it was the verb that seemed more basic):

(41) *Nouns*   *Verbs*
      BATH   BATHE
      BREATH   BREATHE
      HOUSE [...s]   HOUSE [...z]
      WREATH   WREATHE

A meaning for *de-* at (38) is clearly identifiable, namely 'remove X from' (compare its function in deriving verbs from verbs, e.g. DESENSITISE). However, neither *-ise* nor *-ify* has a clearcut meaning apart from its verb-forming function (ORGANISE does not share any obvious element of meaning with ORGAN, for example). The suffixes *-ise* and *-ify* can derive verbs from adjectival bases too, as in NATIONALISE, TENDERISE, INTENSIFY, PURIFY. Hence, when the roots to which they are attached are bound (e.g. CAUTERISE, SANITISE, PETRIFY, SATISFY, MAGNIFY), it is often impossible to decide whether these roots are fundamentally nominal or adjectival. The suffix *-ate* shows the same sort of ambivalence. Words such as GENERATE, ROTATE, REPLICATE and LOCATE clearly contain a root and a suffix, because the same roots crop up elsewhere (e.g. in GENERAL, ROTOR, REPLICA, LOCAL). However, because most of the bases to which *-ate* is attached are bound roots, it does not clearly favour either adjectival or nominal bases.

It will be evident by now that suffixes play a larger role than prefixes in English derivational morphology. But there is still one prefix to be mentioned: *en-* (with its allomorph *em-*), which forms verbs meaning 'cause to become X' or 'cause to possess or enter X' from a few adjectives and nouns: ENFEEBLE, ENSLAVE, EMPOWER, ENRAGE, ENTHRONE, ENTOMB.

With the adjectives BOLD and LIVE as bases, the prefix *en-* is combined with a suffix *-en*: EMBOLDEN, ENLIVEN. This suffix usually occurs without the prefix, however, and does so quite widely (e.g. TIGHTEN, LOOSEN, STIFFEN, WEAKEN, WIDEN, REDDEN, DEEPEN, TOUGHEN). These verbs have either an intransitive meaning, 'become X', or a transitive one, 'cause to become X'. The adjectives that can constitute bases for such verbs share an unusual characteristic, however, which becomes evident when we consider some verbs in *-en* that are imaginable, yet do not occur: *GREENEN, *NARROWEN, *STRONGEN, *TALLEN, *BLUEN, *CLEAREN. It turns out that the adjectives that can be bases for deriving *-en* verbs are all monosyllabic and all end in plosives (the sounds usually spelled *p, b, t, d, (c)k* and *g* in English) or fricatives (including the sounds usually spelled *s, th, f* and *v*). What is wrong with *GREENEN and the other unsuccessful candidates is that their bases end in a sound other than a plosive or a fricative – although with STRONG we get round this restriction (so to speak) by adding *-en* instead to the corresponding noun, STRENGTH (which ends in a fricative sound), so as to yield STRENGTHEN.

Can we then say that all adjectives ending in a plosive or a fricative, or at least a systematically identifiable subset of these adjectives, can be the base for a verb in *-en*? That is a question about productivity, so we will defer it to Chapter 8. However, the starting-point for an answer is to look for adjectives which end in plosives or fricatives but for which there is no corresponding verb in *-en*. There is no need to wait until Chapter 8 before embarking on this search!

5.10 Conclusion: generality and idiosyncrasy

This chapter has illustrated, by no means exhaustively, the wide variety of tasks that derivation can play. In this respect, derivation contrasts with inflection in English. By comparison with most other European languages, such as French and German, English has few inflectional affixes; however, English is at least as rich as French and German in its derivational resources. Some of the reasons for this are historical, and will be discussed in Chapter 9.

Because of the versatility of derivation in English, one might have expected that many of the processes involved would have been sufficiently predictable in both their application and their meaning so that the lexemes thus derived would not count as lexical items. However, only four of the affixes that we have discussed yield large numbers of lexemes that one would not expect to find listed in a dictionary, namely adverb-forming *-ly*, negative adjectival *un-* and nominal *-ness* and *-ing*. It is as if, despite the fact that lexemes are not necessarily lexical items,

there is a deep-seated readiness to allow them to become lexical items –
that is, to treat the products of all derivational processes, even the most
general and semantically predictable ones, as potentially quirky. Why so?
Underlying this puzzle are big questions about the status of the word as
a linguistic unit – questions too big and controversial to be tackled here.
However, more will be said about unpredictability in derivation when
we discuss productivity in Chapter 8.

Exercises

1. Here are nine verbs, each consisting of a prefix and a bound root
(on the basis of the sort of analysis discussed in Chapter 3). What nouns
can be formed from them by suffixation, and how many of these nouns
are lexical items in the sense of Chapter 2 (i.e. are in some way idiosyncratic)?

define	defer	detain
refine	refer	retain
confine	confer	contain

2. Here are ten adjectives. What verbs can be formed from them by
prefixation, suffixation or conversion, and how many of these verbs are
lexical items?

full	poor	long	active	humble
empty	rich	short	national	proud

3. In the chapter, -ism was discussed only as a suffix for deriving nouns
from adjectives. Give examples to show that it can also be used to derive
nouns from other nouns.

4. In the chapter, -ful was discussed only as a suffix for deriving adjectives from nouns. Give examples to show that it can also be used to derive
nouns from other nouns.

5. In the chapter, -ly was discussed only as a suffix for deriving adverbs
from adjectives. Give examples to show that it can also be used to derive
adjectives from nouns and from other adjectives.

6. In the chapter, the suffix -ar, used for deriving adjectives from nouns
or bound roots, was not mentioned. Make a list of six or seven adjectives
with this suffix, and compare them with a similar number of adjectives
formed with -al. Can you identify any phonological characteristic that
the -ar adjectives share?

7. In the chapter, cook was mentioned as a word form that could belong

to either a noun or a verb lexeme. Show that the verbal lexeme is basic and that the nominal one is derived from it, using arguments similar to those used in respect of HOPE and FEAR.

8. Here is a collection of lexemes, prefixes and suffixes. What is the longest word that you can derive by means of them (that is, the word with the largest number of affixes)? (Your answer will probably be one that does not exist in any dictionary, but is readily interpretable on the basis of the base lexeme and the affixes added to it.)

Lexemes	*Prefixes*	*Suffixes*
COMPARTMENT	un-	-al
DOG	de-	-ie (noun-forming: 'little X')
	re-	-y (adjective-forming: 'X-related')
	dis-	-ation
		-ify
		-ish

Recommendations for reading

I have not attempted to supply a complete list of all the derivational resources of English, but rather to discuss a representative sample of them, along with their formal and semantic characteristics. For such a list, see Marchand (1969), who catalogues all prefixes and suffixes in use in mid-twentieth-century English, and also discusses conversion.

Two pioneering works on derivational morphology within modern linguistic theory are Aronoff (1976) and Jackendoff (1975). They deserve high priority for any reader who wants to go beyond introductory texts.

The issue of whether Austronesian or American Pacific coast languages possess a noun–verb distinction lies well outside the scope of an introductory text on English morphology. However, for readers who wish to pursue this matter, two articles that provide an entrée to it are Jelinek and Demers (1994) and Gil (2000).

6 Compound words, blends and phrasal words

6.1 Compounds versus phrases

In the last chapter, we looked at words (that is, lexemes, not word forms) formed from other words, mainly by means of affixes. In this chapter we will look at **compounds**, that is words formed by combining roots, and the much smaller category of **phrasal words**, that is items that have the internal structure of phrases but function syntactically as words. As we will see, some types of compound are much commoner than others. There are also some styles of writing (for example, newspaper headlines) in which compounds are especially frequent. But first we must deal with an issue that has not arisen so far, because until now all the complex words that we have looked at have contained at least one bound morpheme. Roots in English are mostly free rather than bound. How can we tell, then, whether a pair of such roots constitutes a compound word or a phrase, that is a unit of sentence structure rather than a complex word?

A definite answer is not always possible, but there are enough clear cases to show that the distinction between compounds and phrases is valid. Consider the expressions *a green house*, with its literal meaning, and *a greenhouse*, meaning a glass structure (not usually green in colour!) where delicate plants are reared. There is a difference in sound corresponding to the difference in meaning: in the first expression the main stress is on *house*, while in the second the main stress is on *green*. This pattern of semantic contrast between expressions stressed in different places is quite common, as in the following examples:

(1) *black bóard*   *bláckboard*
    'board that is black'   'board for writing on'
(2) *silk wórm*   *sílkworm*
    'worm made of silk (e.g. a soft toy)'   'caterpillar that spins silk'
(3) *hair nét*   *háirnet*
    'net made of hair'   'net for covering hair'

(4) *white hóuse*   *(the) White House*
    'house that is white'   'residence of the US
                                            President'
(5) *toy fáctory*   *tóy factory*
    'factory that is a toy   'factory where toys are made'
    (e.g. in a model city)'

The items on the left in (1)–(5), like *green hóuse*, are phrases, because it is characteristic of phrases in English to be stressed on the last word, unless some contrast is being stated or implied (e.g. *They live in a* white *house, not a* yellow *one!'*). The items on the right, stressed on the first element like *gréenhouse*, are generally classified as compounds – though this stress pattern applies consistently only to compound nouns, not to compounds in other wordclasses.

Apart from stress, a second criterion traditionally used for distinguishing compounds from phrases is semantic: a compound tends to have a meaning that is more or less idiosyncratic or unpredictable. This is true of most of the compounds in (1)–(5). This criterion must be treated with caution, however, because, as we noted in Chapter 2, being semantically unpredictable does not correlate exactly with being a word. All the same, it is true that words are more likely to be lexical items than phrases are, so treating semantic idiosyncrasy as an indicator of compound status will not often be misleading.

All the compounds in (1)–(5) are nouns, and compound nouns are indeed the commonest type of compound in English. We will examine them in detail in later sections. Meanwhile, Sections 6.2 and 6.3 will deal with compound verbs and adjectives.

6.2 Compound verbs

Verbs formed by compounding are much less usual than verbs derived by affixation. Nevertheless, a variety of types exist which may be distinguished according to their structure:

(6) verb–verb (VV): *stir-fry, freeze-dry*
(7) noun–verb (NV): *hand-wash, air-condition, steam-clean*
(8) adjective–verb (AV): *dry-clean, whitewash*
(9) preposition–verb (PV): *underestimate, outrun, overcook*

Only the PV type is really common, however, and some compounds with *under-, over-* and *out-* do not need to be classed as lexical items. For example, *out-* can create a transitive verb meaning 'outdo in Xing' from any verb denoting a competitive or potentially competitive activity (e.g.

outsail, outsing, outswim), while new words with *over-* can also be created freely (e.g. *overpolish, overcriticise, overbleach*).

You will notice that all these compounds have a verb as the rightmost element, and also that, with most of them, the activity denoted by the compound as whole is a variety of the activity denoted by that rightmost element. Let us call these compounds **right-headed**, the rightmost element being the **head**. Most English compounds are right-headed, but not all, as we shall see in Section 6.6.

6.3 Compound adjectives

On the analogy of (6)–(9), here are some examples of right-headed compound adjectives:

(10) noun–adjective (NA): *sky-high, coal-black, oil-rich*
(11) adjective–adjective (AA): *grey-green, squeaky-clean, red-hot*
(12) preposition–adjective (PA): *underfull, overactive*

As with verbs, it is the type with the preposition *over* as its first element that seems most productive, in that new adjectives of this type, with the meaning 'too X', are readily acceptable: for example, *overindignant, oversmooth*. In *overactive* at (12), the head of the compound is the adjective *active* derived from the verb *act* in the fashion described in Section 5.7. In structure, therefore, this adjective is not a mere string of morphemes (*over* + *act* + *-ive*), but rather a nested structure: [over[act-ive]]. More will be said about the implications of this kind of structuring in Chapter 7.

Adjectives with a VA structure, corresponding to the VV verbs at (2), would resemble a hypothetical *'float-light'* 'light enough to float' or *'sing-happy'* 'happy enough to sing'. One actual example is *fail-safe* 'designed to return to a safe condition if it fails or goes wrong'. However, other such compounds scarcely exist, even though it is easy enough to find plausible meanings for them. This reflects the relative reluctance of verbs to participate in compounding generally in English.

All the compounds in (10)–(12) are right-headed. There are also a few compound adjectives that are not right-headed, but we will discuss them along with all headless compounds in Section 6.5.

6.4 Compound nouns

It is with nouns that compounding really comes into its own as a word forming process in English. That is not surprising. Cultural and technical change produces more novel artefacts than novel activities or novel properties. These changes therefore generate new vocabulary needs that (despite the reservations expressed in Chapter 5 about semantic definitions for word classes) are more readily answered by new nouns than by new verbs or adjectives. Examples can be found with each of the other main word classes supplying the left-hand element:

(13) verb–noun (VN): *swearword, drophammer, playtime*
(14) noun–noun (NN): *hairnet, mosquito net, butterfly net, hair restorer*
(15) adjective–noun (AN): *blackboard, greenstone, faintheart*
(16) preposition–noun (PN): *in-group, outpost, overcoat*

All of these have the main stress on the left – a characteristic identified in Section 6.1 as important for distinguishing compound nouns from noun phrases. (The fact that *hair restorer, butterfly net* and *mosquito net* are spelled with a space does not affect the fact that, from the grammatical point of view, they each constitute one complex word.) Most of these are also right-headed, although we will defer further discussion of headedness to Section 6.6.

If you try to think of more examples for the four types at (13)–(16), you will probably find the task easiest for the NN type at (14). In fact, almost any pair of nouns can be juxtaposed in English so as to form a compound or a phrase – provided that there is something that this compound or phrase could plausibly mean. The issue of meaning turns out to play an important part in distinguishing two kinds of NN compound. Consider the four examples at (14). Does each one have a precise interpretation that is clearly the most natural, on the basis of the meanings of their two components? For *hair restorer*, the answer is surely yes: it most naturally denotes a substance for restoring hair growth. On the other hand, for *hairnet, butterfly net* and *mosquito net* the answer is less clear. What tells us that a hairnet is for keeping one's hair in place, while a butterfly net is for catching butterflies and a mosquito net is for keeping mosquitoes away? This information does not reside in the meaning of *net*, nor in the meanings of *hair, butterfly* and *mosquito*. The most that one can conclude from these individual meanings is that each is a net that has something to do with hair, butterflies and mosquitoes respectively. Arriving at the precise meanings of these compounds depends on our knowledge of the world (that some people collect butterflies, and that mosquitoes can carry disease) rather than on purely linguistic knowledge.

The difference in precision with which we can interpret *hair restorer* on the one hand and *hairnet* etc. on the other hinges on the fact that *restorer* in *hair restorer* is derived from a verb (*restore*). Verbs, unlike most nouns and adjectives, impose expectations and requirements on the noun phrases that accompany them in the sentence. For example, with the verb *sleep* we expect to find one noun phrase as subject; with *eat* we expect to find also a noun phrase as object; and with *give* we expect to find, or at least to be able to identify from the context, a third 'indirect object' noun phrase denoting the recipient of the gift. These expected or required nominal concomitants to a verb are called its **arguments**. For present purposes, what matters is that, when the head of a NN compound is derived from a verb, as *restorer* is, the most natural way to interpret the whole compound is quite precise: the first element expresses the object argument of the verb (that is, the person or thing that undergoes the action). For example, an X-restorer, whatever X is, something or someone that restores X.

Here are some more compounds whose second element is derived from a verb:

(17) sign-writer, slum clearance, crime prevention, wish-fulfilment

For all of these, the most natural interpretation is clear. To interpret any of them some other way – for example, to interpret *crime prevention* as meaning not 'prevention of crime' but 'use of crime for preventive purposes' – seems contrived and unnatural.

It is time to introduce some terminology, for convenience. Let us call a NN compound like *hairnet* or *mosquito net*, in which the right-hand noun is not derived from a verb and whose interpretation is therefore not precisely predictable on a purely linguistic basis, a **primary** or **root compound**. (The term 'root compound' is well established but not particularly appropriate, because primary compounds include many, such as *climbing equipment* or *fitness campaigner*, neither of whose components is a root in the sense of Chapter 2.) Let us call a NN compound like *hair restorer* or *slum clearance*, in which the first element is interpreted as the object of the verb contained within the second, a **secondary** or **verbal compound**. (Yet another term sometime used is **synthetic compound**.) Paradoxically, then, although verbs are relatively rare as elements in compounds in English (the *swearword* pattern is unusual), verbal compounds, in the sense just defined, are common.

Secondary compounds are certainly right-headed, in that (for example) *crime prevention* denotes a kind of prevention and *wish-fulfilment* denotes a kind of fulfilment. In this respect they are like most NN compounds and most compounds generally – but not all, as we shall see in the next section.

6.5 Headed and headless compounds

The AN compounds given at (15) included *faintheart* alongside *blackboard* and *greenstone*. However, whereas a greenstone is a kind of stone and a blackboard is a kind of board, a faintheart is not a kind of heart but a kind of person – someone who has a faint heart, metaphorically. So, although *heart* is a noun, it is not appropriate to call *heart* the head of the compound. Rather, *faintheart* is headless, in the sense that its status as a noun is not determined by either of its two components. Similar headless AN compounds are *loudmouth* and *redshank* (a kind of bird that has red legs), and headless NN compounds are *stickleback* (a kind of fish with spines on its back) and *sabretooth*.

A few VN-type compound nouns resemble secondary compounds in that the noun at the right is interpreted as the object of the verb:

(18)   pickpocket, killjoy, cutpurse

These too are headless, in that a pickpocket is not a kind of pocket, for example. An implication of these analyses is as follows: if the fact that *heart* and *pocket* are nouns is really irrelevant to the fact that *faintheart* and *pickpocket* are nouns too, we should expect there to be some headless nouns in which the second element is not a noun at all – and likewise, perhaps, headless adjectives in which the second element is not an adjective. Both expectations turn out to be correct. Some nouns consist of a verb and a preposition or adverb:

(19)   take-off, sell-out, wrap-up, sit-in

In Chapter 5 we saw that nouns are sometimes formed from verbs by conversion, that is with no affix. The nouns at (19) can be seen as a special case of this, where the base is a verb plus another word (sometimes constituting a lexical item), as illustrated in (20):

(20)   a.   The plane took off at noon.
       b.   The chairman wrapped the meeting up.
       c.   The students sat in during the discussion.

As for headless adjectives, there are quite a number consisting of a preposition and a noun:

(21)   overland, in-house, with-profits, offshore, downmarket, upscale, underweight, over-budget

The adjectival status of these compounds can often be confirmed by their appropriateness in comparative contexts and with the modifier *very*:

(22) a. They live in a very downmarket neighbourhood.
  b. This year's expenditure is even more over-budget than last year's.

The fact that the word class of these headless compounds is not determined by any element inside them (that they have no internal 'centre', one might say) has led some grammarians to call them **exocentric** – that is, having a 'centre' outside themselves, figuratively speaking. According to this approach, headed compounds would be regarded as having an internal 'centre'; and, sure enough, they are sometimes called **endocentric**.

6.6 Blends and acronyms

In all the examples that we have examined so far, the whole of each component root (or base) is reproduced in the compound. Sporadically, however, we encounter a kind of compound where at least one component is reproduced only partially. These are known as **blends**. A straightforward example is *smog*, blended from *smoke* and *fog*; a more elaborate one is *chortle* (first used by Lewis Carroll in *Through the Looking Glass*), blended from *chuckle* and *snort*.

Examples of partial blends, where only one component is truncated, are *talkathon* (from *talk* plus *marathon*) and *cheeseburger* (from *cheese* plus *hamburger*). The ready acceptance of *cheeseburger* and similar blends such as *beefburger* and *vegeburger* may have been encouraged by a feeling that *hamburger* is a compound whose first element is *ham* – scarcely appropriate semantically, since the meat in a hamburger (originally a kind of meat pattie from Hamburg) is beef.

The most extreme kind of truncation that a component of a blend can undergo is reduction to just one sound (or letter), usually the first. Blends made up of initial letters are known as **acronyms**, of which well-known examples are *NATO* (for *North Atlantic Treaty Organisation*), *ANZAC* (for *Australian and New Zealand Army Corps*), *RAM* (for *random access memory*), *SCSI* (pronounced *scuzzy*, from *small computer systems interface*), and *AIDS* (from *acquired immune deficiency syndrome*). Intermediate between an acronym and a blend is *sonar* (from *sound navigation and ranging*).

The use of capital letters in the spelling of some of these words reflects the fact that speakers are aware of their acronym status. It does not follow that any string of capital letters represents an acronym. If the conventional way of reading the string is by pronouncing the name of each letter in turn, as with *USA* and *RP* (standing for the 'Received Pronunciation' of British English), then it is not an acronym but an abbreviation.

It is clear from these examples that blending and acronymy are in active use for the creation of new vocabulary. However, they differ from derivational affixation and normal compounding in being more or less self-conscious, and are concentrated in areas where the demand for new noun vocabulary is greatest, such as (currently) information technology.

6.7 Compounds containing bound combining forms

Most of the compounds that we have looked at so far involve roots that are free forms. But the vocabulary of English, especially in scientific and technical areas, includes a huge repertoire of compounds that are made up of bound roots, known as **combining forms**, already alluded to in Chapter 3. Here are just a few:

(23) anthropology, sociology, cardiogram, electrocardiogram, retro-grade, retrospect, plantigrade

For most of these, the meaning of the whole is clearly determinable from that of the parts: for example, *anthrop(o)-* 'human' plus *-(o)logy* 'science or study' yields a word that means 'science or study of human beings', and *planti-* 'sole (of foot)' and *-grade* 'walking' yields a word meaning 'walking on the soles of the feet'. This semantic predictability is crucial to the coining of new technical terms using these elements.

Apart from containing bound roots, *anthropology* differs in two other ways from most compound nouns. Firstly, it has a central linking vowel *-o-* that cannot conclusively be assigned to either root. In this respect it resembles many combining-form compounds. Secondly, although it is a noun, its stress is not on the first element – unless the linking *-o-* belongs there. In this respect it resembles e.g. *monogamy, philosophy* and *aristocracy*.

In Chapters 3 and 5 we encountered bound roots that could function as the base for derivational affixation, such as *aud-* in *audible, audition* etc. Not surprisingly, some combining forms can function in this way too (in other words, the dividing line between combining forms and other bound roots is not sharp): for example, *soci-* and *electr(o)-* from (23) also occur, indeed much more commonly, in *social* and *electric*.

Given that combining forms, and the compounds that contain them, are so untypical of compounds in general, it is natural to ask how English has come to acquire them. In fact, they come mostly from Greek or Latin, through deliberate borrowings to supply new needs for technical vocabulary that arose partly from the revival of learning in western Europe in the fifteenth and sixteenth centuries known as the Renais-sance, and partly from the industrial revolution of the eighteenth century and its scientific spin-offs. We will have more to say about these circumstances in Chapter 9.

6.8 Phrasal words

In some of the compounds that we have looked at so far, relationships are expressed that are the same as ones expressed in syntax: for example, the verb–object relationship between *hair* and *restore* in *hair restorer*. On the other hand, the way in which the verb–object relationship is expressed in this compound is quite different from how it is expressed in syntax, in that the two words appear in the opposite order: we say *This substance restores hair*, not **This substance hair-restores*. There is a clear difference between compound word structure and sentence structure here. But there are also complex items that function as words, yet whose internal structure is that of a clause or phrase rather than of a compound. There is no standard term for these items, so I will introduce the term **phrasal words**.

An example of a phrasal word is the noun *jack-in-the-box*. Structurally this has the appearance of a noun phrase in which the head noun, *jack*, is modified by a prepositional phrase, *in the box*, exactly parallel to the phrases *people in the street* or *(a) book on the shelf*. However, it forms its plural by suffixing -*s* not to the head noun (as in *books on the shelf*) but to the whole expression: not '*jacks-in-the-box*' but *jack-in-the-boxes*, as in *They jumped up and down like jack-in-the-boxes*. Though structurally a phrase, then, it behaves as a word. Contrast this with another item which is at least as idiosyncratic in meaning and which has a superficially similar structure: *brother-in-law*. A crucial difference is that *brother-in-law* forms its plural by affixing -*s* not to the whole expression but to the head noun: *brothers-in-law*. Despite its hyphens, therefore, *brother-in-law* is not a word at all but a phrase (although also a lexical item – a combination discussed in Chapter 2).

Can phrases other than noun phrases constitute phrasal words? The answer is yes. Adjectival examples are *dyed-in-the-wool* (as in *a dyed-in-the-wool Republican*) or *couldn't-care-less* (as in *a couldn't-care-less attitude*). Syntactically, *dyed-in-the-wool* looks like an adjective phrase consisting of an adjective (*died* 'artificially coloured') modified by a prepositional phrase, just like *suitable for the party* or *devoted to his children*. However, such a phrase cannot entirely precede the noun it modifies (we say *a man devoted to his children* or *suitable music for the party*, not **a devoted to his children man* or **suitable for the party music*); therefore the behaviour of *dyed-in-the-wool* is that of a word rather than a phrase. As for *couldn't-care-less*, its structure is that of a verb phrase, but again its behaviour is that of an adjective (e.g. *Your attitude is even more couldn't-care-less than hers!*).

This seems an appropriate point to mention a small and rather old-fashioned class of lexical items exemplified by *governor general, attorney general, court martial* and *lord lieutenant.* How do they form their plural: like *attorney generals*, or like *attorneys general?* If you prefer the former, then these items may seem at first like further phrasal words – except for the fact that they differ from normal English noun phrases in having an adjective following the noun rather than preceding it. It seems better, therefore, to treat them as examples of something that we have not so far encountered: endocentric words which, untypically, have their head on the left rather than on the right. On the other hand, if you prefer the latter sort of plural (*attorneys general*), they seem more akin to *brother(s)-in-law*: not words but lexicalised phrases. If, finally, neither kind of plural sounds quite right to you, that is not surprising, because however these items are analysed, their structure is unusual.

6.9 Conclusion

This chapter has illustrated various ways in which an English word may itself be composed of words. In Chapter 7 I will have more to say about a fact that I have not emphasised so far: one or both of the component words in a compound may itself be a compound, so there is in principle no upper limit to the size of compounds. We have also seen that at least one syntactic relationship can be expressed within compounds just as well as within sentences, namely the verb–object relationship (or perhaps one should say the action–goal relationship), as in *hair restorer.* One might ask, then, why English, or any language, needs both compound word-structure and clause-structure side by side: could not just one do the work performed in actual English by both? That is an important question, but unfortunately one for which there is no generally agreed answer. Further discussion of it is therefore a task for research papers, rather than for an introductory textbook such as this.

Exercises

1. Which of the following are compound words, which are phrases, and which are phrasal words?

   (a) *moonlight, moonscape, harvest moon, blue moon* (as in *once in a blue moon*)
   (b) *blueberry, bluebottle, greybeard, sky-blue, blue-pencil* (as in *they blue-pencilled the script heavily*)
   (c) *pencil case, eyebrow pencil, pencil sharpener, pencil-thin, thin air* (as in *they vanished into thin air*)

(d) *airport, Royal Air Force, air conditioning, Air France*
(e) *silkworm, silk shirt, T-shirt*
(f) *stick-in-the-mud, lady-in-waiting, forget-me-not, has-been, wannabe*
(g) *overrún* (verb), *óverrun* (noun, as in *in a big cost overrun*), *undercoat* (noun), *undercoat* (verb, as in *We undercoated the walls in white*), *underhand, handover*

2. Of the compounds (not the phrases or phrasal words) in Exercise 1, which are endocentric and which are exocentric?

3. Of the compound nouns in Exercise 1, which are primary (or root) compounds and which are secondary (or verbal) compounds?

4. Identify (with the help of a dictionary, if necessary) the sources of the following blends or acronyms: *brunch, motel, radar, modem, laser.*

5. Each of these words is a compound containing at least one bound Graeco-Latin combining form. With the help of a dictionary if necessary, identify a meaning for each such combining form, and find another word that contains it:

   nanosecond, protoplasm, endocentric, polyphony, leucocyte, omnivorous, octahedron

Recommendations for reading

On compounding, see Adams (1973) for a description of the varieties that occur and Selkirk (1982) for a more theoretically adventurous, though now somewhat dated, discussion. Be warned, however, that these writers treat as compounds some noun–noun collocations that I analyse as phrases. One reason seems to be that they, like many linguists, are reluctant to analyse nouns as modifiers (like adjectives) within a phrase, so that they are prevented from distinguishing structurally (as I do) between the compound *tóy factory* ('factory for making toys') and the phrase *toy fáctory* ('factory which is a toy'). A similar view is taken by Bauer (1998), who cites, for example, the apparent arbitrariness of treating *apple píe* (with stress on the second element) as a phrase, if *ápple cake* (with stress on the first element) is a compound. Also, some writers blur the difference in status between lexemes and lexical items, discussed in Chapter 2, and hence analyse as a compound word any noun-noun collocation with an idiosyncratic meaning, such as *spaghetti wéstern*.
   The view that there is really no fundamental difference between word-structure and sentence-structure – a view that blurs fundamentally the distinction between compounds and phrases – is espoused by

Lieber (1992). However, this is not the dominant view among contemporary morphologists. For an opposed view, see Anderson (1992), reviewed by Carstairs-McCarthy (1993).

A classic discussion of secondary compounds is Lieber (1983). See also section 4.4 in Carstairs-McCarthy (1992).

7 A word and its structure

7.1 Meaning and structure

In Chapter 2 it was pointed out that many words have meanings that are predictable, more or less, on the basis of their components. Some words are so predictable, indeed, that they do not have to be listed as lexical items. This predictability of meaning depends on how the structure of complex word forms guides their interpretation. Even with words that are lexically listed, unless their meaning is entirely different from what one might expect, such guidance is relevant. This chapter is about how it operates, and also (in Section 7.5) about circumstances under which meaning and structure appear to diverge.

In some words, structure is straightforward. For example, the lexeme HELPFUL, already discussed in Chapter 5, is derived from the noun base HELP by means of the adjective-forming suffix -ful. Because there are only two elements in this word form, it may seem there is not much to say about its structure. Even with just these two components, however, there is clearly a distinction between the actual word form *helpful* and the ill-formed one *-ful-help* – a distinction that will be discussed in Section 7.2. Sections 7.3 and 7.4 deal with affixed words and compounds that have more than two components, such as *unhelpfulness* and *car insurance premium*. Finally, in Section 7.5, we will confront a dilemma posed by items like *French history teacher* in its two interpretations ('French teacher of history' and 'teacher of French history').

7.2 Affixes as heads

Chapter 5 showed how, in English derivational morphology, suffixes heavily outnumber prefixes. In Chapter 6 we saw that most compounds are headed, with the head on the right. Superficially these two facts are unconnected. Consider, however, the role played by the head *house* of a compound such as *greenhouse*. As head, *house* determines the compound's syntactic status (as a noun), and also its meaning, inasmuch as a green-house is a kind of house for plants. This is very like the role played by the suffix -*er* in the derived word *teacher*: it determines that *teacher* is a noun, unlike its base, the verb *teach*, and it contributes the meaning 'someone who Xs', where the semantic blank X is here filled in by *teach*. Many (though not all) linguists therefore treat -*er* as the head of *teacher* in just the same way as *house* is the head of *greenhouse*. This is relevant to the distinction between *helpful* and **-ful-help*. In *helpful*, the affix is what determines that the whole word is an adjective, and so counts as its head. Accordingly, **-ful-help* violates English expectations not just because the affix is on the wrong side, but also because the rightmost element is not the head. In the derived words *teacher* and *helpful*, therefore, the two components are not equal contributors, so to speak; rather, the righthand element (as in most compounds) has a special status.

Superficially, this view of affixes as heads leads us to expect that prefixed words should be as rare in English as left-headed compounds are (items such as *attorney general*). Yet prefixes, though fewer than suffixes, include some that are of very common occurrence, such as *un-* 'not' and *re-* 'again'. Is our expectation disappointed, then? Not really, despite first appearances. Consider the relationship between *helpful* and *unhelpful*. In *helpful*, -*ful* has a clearly wordclass-determining role because it changes a noun, *help*, into an adjective. In *unhelpful*, however, *un-* has no such role; rather, it leaves the wordclass of *helpful* unchanged (see Section 5.6). This characteristic of *un-* is not restricted to adjectives, moreover. Verbs to which *un-* is prefixed remain verbs (e.g. *untie, unfasten, unclasp*), and those few nouns to which *un-* is prefixed remain nouns (*unease, unrest*). This strongly suggests that the head of of all these words is not *un-* but the base to which *un-* is attached (*helpful, tie, ease* etc.) – and which is the righthand element.

Similar arguments apply to *re-*: *rearrange, repaint* and *re-educate* are verbs, just as *arrange, paint* and *educate* are. These prefixed verbs, there-fore, are right-headed also. The only prefixes that are unequivocally heads are those that change wordclass, such as *de-* in *delouse* (deriving verbs from nouns) and *en-* in *enfeeble* and *enslave* (deriving verbs from nouns and adjectives) (see Section 5.9). So, while left-headed derived words do exist, just as left-headed compounds do, they are also not so numerous as may at first appear.

7.3 More elaborate word forms: multiple affixation

Many derived words contain more than one affix. Examples are *unhelp-fulness* and *helplessness*. Imagine now that the structure of these words is entirely 'flat': that is, that they each consist of merely a string of affixes plus a root, no portions of the string being grouped together as a substring or smaller constituent within the word. An unfortunate consequence of that analysis is that it would complicate considerably what needs to be said about the behaviour of the suffixes *-ful* and *-less*. In Chapter 5 these were straightforwardly treated as suffixes that attach to nouns to form adjectives. However, if the nouns *unhelpfulness* and *helplessness* are flat-structured, we must also allow *-ful* and *-less* to appear internally in a string that constitutes a noun – but not just anywhere in such a string, because (for example) the imaginary nouns **sadlessness* and **meanlessingness*, though they contain *-less*, are nevertheless not words, and (one feels) could never be words.

The flat-structure approach misses a crucial observation. *Unhelpfulness* contains the suffix *-ful* only by virtue of the fact that it contains (in some sense) the adjective *helpful*. Likewise, *helplessness* contains *-less* by virtue of the fact that it contains *helpless*. Once that is recognised, the apparent need to make special provision for *-ful* and *-less* when they appear inside complex words, rather than as their rightmost element, disappears. In fact, both these words can be seen as built up from the root *help* by successive processes of affixation (with N, V and A standing for noun, verb and adjective respectively):

(1) *help*N + *-ful* → *helpful*A
    un- + *helpful* → *unhelpful*A
    unhelpful + *-ness* → *unhelpfulness*N

(2) *help*N + *-less* → *helpless*A
    helpless + *-ness* → *helplessness*N

Another way of representing this information is in terms of a branching **tree diagram**, as in (3) and (4), which also represent the fact that the noun *help* is formed by conversion from the verb:

(3)

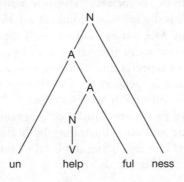

(4)

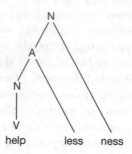

help   less   ness

(The term 'tree diagram' is odd, because the 'branches' point downwards, more like roots than branches! However, this topsy-turvy usage has become well established in linguistic discussions.) The points in a tree diagram from which branches sprout are called **nodes**. The nodes in (3) and (4) are all labelled, to indicate the wordclass of the string (that is, of the part of the whole word) that is dominated by the node in question. For example, the second-to-top node in (3) is labelled 'A' to indicate that the string *unhelpful* that it dominates is an adjective, while the topmost node is labelled 'N' because the whole word is a noun. The information about structure contained in tree diagrams such as (3) and (4) can also be conveyed in a **labelled bracketing**, where one pair of brackets corresponds to each node in the tree: [[un-[[help$_V$]$_N$-ful]$_A$]$_A$-ness]$_N$, [[[help$_V$]$_N$-less]$_A$-ness]$_N$.

One thing stands out about all the nodes in (3) and (4): each has no more than two branches sprouting downwards from it. This reflects the fact that, in English, derivational processes operate by adding no more than one affix to a base – unlike languages where material may be added simultaneously at both ends, constituting what is sometimes called a **circumfix**. English possesses no uncontroversial examples of circumfixes, and branching within word-structure tree diagrams is never more than **binary** (i.e. with two branches). (The only plausible candidate for a circumfix in English is the *en-* ... *-en* combination that forms *enliven* and *embolden* from *live* and *bold*; but *en-* and *-en* each appears on its own too, e.g. in *enfeeble* and *redden*, so an alternative analysis as a combination of a prefix and a suffix seems preferable.) The single branch connecting N to V above *help* in (3) and (4) reflects the fact that the noun *help* is derived from the verb *help* by conversion, with no affix.

At (5) and (6) are two more word tree diagrams, incorporating an adverbial (Adv) node and also illustrating both affixal and non-affixal heads, each italicised element being the head of the constituent dominated by the node immediately above it:

(5)

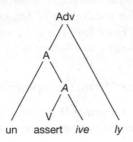

(6)

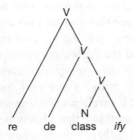

Some complex words contain elements about which one may reasonably argue whether they are complex or not. For example, the word *reflection* is clearly divisible into a base *reflect* and a suffix *-ion*; but does *reflect* itself consist of one morpheme or two? This kind of uncertainty was discussed in Chapter 2. But, if we put it on one side, then any complex word form consisting of a free root and affixes turns out to be readily analysable in the simple fashion illustrated here, with binary branching and with either the affix or the base as the head. (I say 'free root' rather than 'root' only because some bound roots are hard to assign to a wordclass: for example, *matern-* in *maternal* and *maternity*.)

Another salient point in all of (3)–(6) is that more than one node in a tree diagram may carry the same wordclass label (N, V, A). At first sight, this may not seem particularly remarkable. However, it has considerable implications for the size of the class of all possible words in English. Linguists are fond of pointing out that there is no such thing as the longest sentence of English (or of any language), because any candidate for longest-sentence status can be lengthened by embedding it in a context such as *Sharon says that* ___. One cannot so easily demonstrate that there is no such thing as the longest word in English; but it is not necessary to do so in order to demonstrate the versatility and vigour of English word-formation processes. Given that we can find nouns inside nouns, verbs inside verbs, and so on, it is hardly surprising that (as was shown in Chapter 2) the vocabulary of English, or of any individual speaker, is not a closed, finite list. The issue of how new words can be formed will be taken up again in Chapter 8.

7.4 More elaborate word forms: compounds within compounds

In the previous section, we saw that the structure of words derived by affixation can be represented in tree diagrams where each branch has at most two branches. The same applies to compounds: any compound has just two immediate constituents. In Chapter 6, all the compounds that were discussed contained just two parts. This was not an accident or an arbitrary restriction. To see this, consider for example the noun that one might use to denote a new cleaning product equally suitable for ovens and windows. Parallel to the secondary compound *hair restorer* are the two two-part compounds *oven cleaner* and *window cleaner*. Can we then refer to the new product with a three-part compound such as *window oven cleaner*? The answer is surely no. *Window oven cleaner* is not naturally interpreted to mean something that cleans both windows and ovens; rather, it means something that cleans window ovens (that is, ovens that have a see-through panel in the door). This is a clue that its structure is not as in (7) but as in (8):

(7)

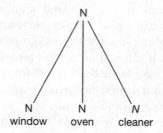

(8)

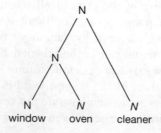

The structure at (8) seems appropriate even for complex compounds such as *verb–noun contrasts* and *Reagan–Gorbachev encounters*. As simple compounds, *verb–noun* and *Regan–Gorbachev* certainly sound odd. Nevertheless *verb–noun contrasts* denotes crucially contrasts between verbs and nouns, not contrasts some of which involve verbs and others of which involve nouns; therefore *verb–noun* deserves to be treated as a subunit within the whole compound *verb–noun contrast*. Likewise, a Reagan–Gorbachev encounter necessarily involves both Reagan and Gorbachev, not just one of the two, so *Reagan–Gorbachev* deserves to be treated as a subunit within *Reagan–Gorbachev encounters*.

In Chapter 6 we concentrated on compounds with only two members. But, given that a compound is a word and that compounds contain words, it makes sense that, in some compounds, one or both of the components should itself be a compound – and (8), with its most natural interpretation, shows that this is indeed possible, at least with compound nouns. Moreover, the compound at (8) can itself be an element in a larger compound, such as the one at (9) meaning 'marketing of a product for cleaning window ovens':

(9)

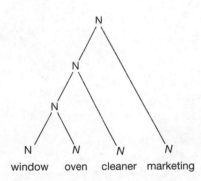

At this point, it is worth pausing to consider whether these more elaborate examples comply with what was said in Section 6.1 about where stress is placed within compound nouns. *Window oven*, if it is a compound, should have its main stress on the lefthand element, namely *window* – and that seems correct. The same applies to *window oven cleaner*: its main stress should be on *window oven*, and specifically on its lefthand element, namely *window*. Again, that seems correct. So we will predict that the whole compound at (9) should have its main stress on the lefthand element too – a prediction that is again consistent with how I, as a native speaker, find it most natural to pronounce this complex word. It is true that other elements than *window* can be emphasised for the sake of contrast: for example, I can envisage a context at a conference of sales executives where one might say *We are concerned with window oven cleaner márketing today, not with manufácture.* Nevertheless, where no contrast is implied or stated (such as between marketing and manufacture), the most natural way of pronouncing the example at (9) renders *window* the most prominent element.

Can we then conclude that all complex compound nouns follow the left-stressed pattern of simple compound nouns? Before saying yes, we need to make sure that we have examined all relevant varieties. It may have struck you that, in (8) and (9), the compounds-within-compounds are uniformly on the left. We have not yet looked at compounds (or potential compounds) in which it is the righthand element (in fact, the head) that is a compound. Consider the following examples:

(10)   (11)

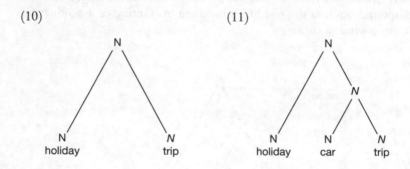

(12)

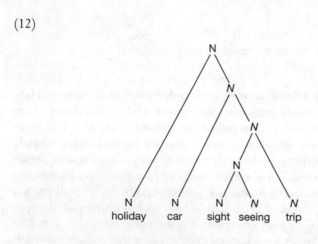

Native speakers are likely to agree sith me that, whereas in (10) the main stress is on *holiday*, in (11) it is on *car*. (Again, we are assuming that no contrast is implied – between a holiday trip and a business trip, say.) This is consistent with *car trip* being a compound with *car* as its lefthand element, but not (at first sight) with an analysis in which *holiday car trip* is a compound noun with *holiday* as its lefthand element. The stress on the righthand element in *holiday car trip* makes it resemble phrases such as *green hóuse* and *toy fáctory*, discussed in Section 6.1, rather than compounds such as *gréenhouse* and *tóy factory*. Yet it would be strange if a compound noun cannot itself be the head of a compound noun, given that any other kind of noun can be.

The best solution seems to be to qualify what was said in Chapter 6 about stress in compound nouns. The usual pattern, with stress on the left, is overridden if the head is a compound. In that case, stress is on the right – that is, on the compound which constitutes the head. Another way of expressing this is to say that the righthand component in a compound noun gets stressed if and only if it is itself a compound; otherwise, the lefthand component gets stressed. This is consistent with the examples in Chapter 6 as well as with native speakers' intuitions about pairs such as (10) and (11). It is also consistent with a more complex example such as (12), involving internal compounds on both left and right branches. If you apply carefully to (12) the formula that we have arrived at, you should find that it predicts that the main stress should be on *sight* – which seems correct.

7.5 Apparent mismatches between meaning and structure

Earlier, the point was made that the reliable interpretation of complex words (whether derived or compounded) depends on an expectation that meaning should go hand in hand with structure. So far, this expectation has been fulfilled (provided we ignore words with totally idiosyncratic meanings). The meaning of a complex whole such as *unhelpfulness* or *holiday car trip* is built up out of the meanings of its two constituent parts, which in turn are built up out of the meanings of their parts, and so on until we reach individual morphemes, which by definition are semantically indivisible. In this section, however, we will discuss a few instances where this expectation is not fulfilled. Discussing these instances leads us to the question of whether a unit larger than a word (that is, a phrase) can ever be a constituent of a compound word. There is no agreed answer to these questions, but the kinds of English expression that give rise to them are sufficiently common that they cannot be ignored, even in an introductory textbook.

Consider the expression *nuclear physicist*. Its structure seems clear: it is a phrase consisting of two words, an adjective *nuclear* and a noun *physicist*. So, if the interpretation of linguistic expressions is always guided by their structure, it ought to mean a physicist who is nuclear. Yet that is wrong: a physicist is a person, and it makes no sense to describe a person as 'nuclear'. Instead, this expression means someone who is an expert in nuclear physics. So we have a paradox: in terms of morphology and syntax, the structure of the expression can be represented by the bracketing [[nuclear] [physicist]], but from the semantic point of view a more appropriate structure seems to be [[nuclear physic-]-ist]. We thus have what has come to be called a **bracketing paradox**. In this instance, the meaning seems to direct us towards an analysis in which the suffix *-ist* is attached not to a word or root but to a phrase, *nuclear physics*. Is it possible, then, for a word to be formed by adding an affix not to another word but to a phrase?

A similar problem is presented by the expression *French historian*. This has two interpretations: 'historian who is French' and 'expert in French history (not necessarily a French person)'. The first interpretation presents no difficulty: it is the interpretation that we expect if we analyse *French historian* as a phrase, just like *green house* (as opposed to *greenhouse*). This implies a structure [[French] [historian]]. However, the second interpretation seems to imply a structure [[French histori-]-an], in which a phrase is combined with an affix. We are faced with a dilemma. Should we acknowledge the second structure as the basis for the second interpretation? Or should we say that, with both interpretations, the structure of the expression is the same (namely [[French] [historian]]), but that for one of the interpretations this structure is a bad guide? Without putting forward a 'right answer', I will mention two further observations that must be taken into account – two observations that, it must be said, pull in opposite directions.

Examples of other adjective–noun combinations whose meanings diverge from their structure are *plastic surgeon* (denoting not a kind of doll, but an expert in cosmetic surgery) and *chemical engineer* (denoting an expert in chemical engineering, not a person who is 'chemical'). These differ from *nuclear physicist*, however, in that there is no way of bracketing them so as to yield a structure that corresponds closely to the meaning. So, even if the meaning of *nuclear physicist* can be handled by the paradoxical bracketing [[nuclear physic-]-ist], no such device is available for *plastic surgeon* and *chemical engineer*. This means that some other way of reconciling their structure–meaning divergence must be found. It does not matter for present purposes how that reconciliation is achieved. What does matter is that, however it is achieved, the same method will presumably be available to handle *nuclear physicist*, and also *French historian* in the sense 'expert in French history'. This weakens the argument for recognising a 'semantic' bracketing distinct from the 'grammatical' one. Rather, we can simply say that, for example, [[French] [historian]], so structured, has two interpretations.

Those examples all involve derivation. What about any apparent bracketing paradoxes involving compounding? Consider the item *French history teacher*. In the sense 'French teacher of history', this is a phrase consisting of an adjective and a noun, just like *French painter*, the only difference being that the noun in *French history teacher* is the compound *history teacher*, just like the noun *portrait painter* in *French portrait painter*. But what about the interpretation 'teacher of French history'? Is this a compound noun with the structure [[French history] teacher]? The trouble with that analysis is that *French history*, with its stress on *history*, seems clearly to be a phrase, not a word; yet, if a phrase such as *French history* is permitted to appear as a component of a compound word, we are faced with explaining why phrases cannot appear inside compounds generally – why, that is, we do not encounter compounds such as *eventful history teacher*, with the phrase *eventful history* as its first element, and with the meaninging 'teacher of eventful history', or *history skilled teacher*, with the phrase *skilled teacher* as its head. Perhaps, then, we should say of *French history teacher* essentially the same as what was suggested concerning *French historian*: it has only one structure, that of a phrase ([French [history teacher]]), even though it has two interpretations, one of which diverges from that structure.

Some implications of that analysis are unwelcome, however. Consider the expressions *fresh áir fanatic* and *open dóor policy*. Their main stress is on *air* and *door*, as indicated, and their meanings are 'fanatic for fresh air' and 'policy of maintaining an open door (to immigration, for example)'. These are parallel to the meaning 'teacher of French history', which, we have suggested, diverges from its structure [French [history teacher]]. But, whereas *French history teacher* has a second meaning that corresponds exactly to that structure, *fresh áir fanatic* and *open dóor policy* have no such second meaning; one cannot interpret them as meaning 'fresh fanatic for air' or 'open policy about doors'. So a bracketing such as [fresh [air fanatic]] would diverge not just from one of the meanings of *fresh air fanatic*, but from its only meaning!

A clue to a way out of this problem lies in comparing the actual expressions at (13) with the non-existent or ill-formed ones in (14):

(13) a. *fresh air fanatic*
     b. *open door policy*

    c. *French historian* 'expert in French history'
    d. *nuclear physicist*
    e. *sexually transmitted disease clinic*
(14) a. *cool air fanatic* 'fanatic for cool air'
    b. *wooden door policy* 'policy on wooden doors'
    c. *suburban historian* 'expert on the history of suburbs'
    d. *recent physicist* 'expert on recent physics' (not 'recent expert on physics')
    e. *easily transmitted disease clinic*

The phrases *fresh air* and *cool air* differ in that *fresh air* is a cliché, even if not precisely an idiom; that is, *fresh air* recurs in a number of stock expressions such as *get/need some fresh air* and *get out into the fresh air*, whereas there are no such stock expressions containing *cool air*. Similarly, *French history* is a cliché in that the history of France is a recognised specialism among historians; on the other hand, the history of suburbs is not recognised as a specialism to the same degree, so the phrase *suburban history*, though perfectly easy to interpret, is not a cliché. The same goes for *open door* versus *wooden door*, *nuclear physics* versus *recent physics*, and *sexually transmitted disease* versus *easily transmitted disease*; the first expression in each pair is an idiom or cliché, while the second is not. What we need to say, it seems, is that a phrase can form part of a compound or derived word provided that the phrase is lexicalised or in some degree institutionalised, so as to become a cliché.

From the point of view of the distinction carefully drawn in Chapter 2 between lexical items and words, this is a surprising conclusion. On the basis of the facts examined in Chapter 2, it seemed that there was no firm link between lexical listing and grammatical structure. Now it appears that that view must be qualified: lexically listed phrases (i.e. idioms) or institutionalised ones (i.e. clichés) can appear in some contexts where unlisted phrases cannot. Whether we should analyse these contexts as being at the word level, so as to treat *nuclear physicist* and *fresh air fanatic* as words rather than phrases, is an issue that beginning students of word-structure should be aware of but need not have an opinion about.

7.6 Conclusion: structure as guide but not straitjacket

It is not surprising that the structure of complex words should guide us in their interpretation. What is perhaps surprising is the uniformity of this structure in English: no node ever has more than two branches, and the element on the righthand branch (whether a root, an affix or a word) is usually the head. What is more, the freedom with which complex structures can be embedded in larger complex structures, especially within compounds, provides great scope for the generation of new words; and, since lexical items are typically though not universally words, this freedom facilitates vocabulary expansion too – an issue that we will take up again in the next chapter.

Despite the general conformity of meaning with structure, there are occasions where meaning gets the upper hand, so to speak. French history and nuclear physics being institutionalised domains of study, we need terms to denote the people who engage in them; and, since the words *historian* and *physicist* exist, *French historian* and *nuclear physicist* come readily to hand as labels for the relevant specialists. This seems a good way to make sense of the mismatches discussed in Section 7.5. However these examples are to be analysed structurally, their existence seems to show that, in derivation and compounding as well as in inflection, semantic pressures can sometimes enforce the existence of an expression with a certain meaning, and the expression chosen for that meaning need not be structurally ideal. The language's acceptance of this expression, nevertheless, shows that, although word-structure guides interpretation, it does not dictate it.

Exoroiooo

1. Draw tree diagrams to illustrate the structure of the following words, assigning appropriate word class labels (N, A or V) to the roots and to the nodes in the trees, and identifying heads:

greediness   cabin crew
deconsecration   cabin crew training
incorruptibility   cabin crew safety training
enthronement   cabin crew safety training manual
re-uncover   airline cabin crew safety training manual
redecompartmentalisation (*an example from Exercise 8 in Chapter 5*)

2. Compare the structure of *unhappiness* and *unhappiest*. Does either of them show a mismatch between meaning and structure?

3. Discuss the grammatical structure of the following, and whether each one is a phrase or a compound word:

income tax rate
high tax rate
value added tax
goods and services tax

Recommendations for reading

The kind of tree diagram that I present is standard in most theoretically oriented discussions of word-structure. The view that affixes can be heads of words is defended by Lieber (1992). The generalisation suggested here about how complex compounds are stressed is drawn from a classic article on 'metrical phonology' by Liberman and Prince (1977). For an introduction to this aspect of phonology, see Hogg and McCully (1987).

On bracketing paradoxes, much the best discussion (in my view) is that of Spencer (1988).

8 Productivity

8.1 Introduction: kinds of productivity

Tesxtbooks on linguistics, and particularly on word structure, usually introduce at an early stage a distinction between 'productive' and 'unproductive' word formation processes. Some readers of this book may wonder why I have not done so before now, especially when discussing criteria for determining which words are lexical items (Chapter 2), or the variety of plural and past tense forms in English (Chapter 4). The reason why I have avoided the term so far is that 'productivity' is used to mean a variety of different things, and it seemed best to avoid the term entirely until any potential confusions could be resolved – a task for this chapter. This risk of confusion does not mean that the notion of productivity is unhelpful. On the contrary, once the various senses are teased apart, the outcome turns out to shed light on the relationship between word formation and lexical listing, and to highlight an important respect in which word-structure differs from sentence-structure.

Productivity is closely tied to regularity, but regularity in shape has to be distinguished from regularity in meaning. These are dealt with in Sections 8.2 and 8.3 respectively. One aspect of vocabulary in English and perhaps in all languages is a dislike of exact synonyms, and the implications of this for word formation is discussed in Section 8.4. Section 8.5 deals with some semantic implications of the freedom with which compound nouns are formed in English. Numerical measures of productivity are touched on in Section 8.6. Finally, Section 8.7 draws attention to the lack of any comparable notion in syntax.

8.2 Productivity in shape: formal generality and regularity

In earlier chapters we have observed that some processes of inflection and derivation are more widely used than others. For example, among ways of forming abstract nouns from adjectives, *-ness* (as in *greyness, happiness, richness*) is more widely used than *-ity* (as in *sensitivity, purity*) or *-th* (as in *depth, length*). I will use *-ness, -ity* and *-th* to tease apart different ways in which a process can be 'productive'.

The suffix *-ness* is **formally general** in the sense that, when attached to most adjectives, it yields an abstract noun which is either in common use (*greyness, richness* etc.) or would not need to be listed as a lexical item because its existence is predictable, given the existence of the adjective. Thus, once one has learned the existence and meaning of the adjective *dioecious*, one does not have to learn separately the existence of a noun *dioeciousness*. (*Dioeciousness* thus resembles the adverb *dioeciously*, discussed in Chapter 2.) The suffix *-ness* is also **formally regular**, in the sense that one can specify what sort of structure an adjective must have in order to be a possible base for it – namely, any structure whatever. That is, whatever adjective *-ness* is attached to, the result sounds like a possible noun, even though it may not be one that is conventionally used (e.g. *sensitiveness, pureness, longness*). If native English speakers hear a non-English-speaker use the word *longness* instead of *length*, they will almost certainly be able to understand what the speaker means, even if *longness* is not a word that they themselves would use.

By contrast, both *-ity* and *-th* are much less general. With most adjectives, the result of attaching either of these is something that is not only not an actual noun but also not a possible noun. For example, **greyth* and **richity* sound not merely unconventional but positively un-English; by contrast with *longness*, they are not words that we would understand without effort in the unlikely event of our hearing them used. But this does not mean that both these suffixes are equally irregular. In fact, *-ity* is formally quite regular, in the sense that possible bases for it are easy to specify: adjectives in *-ive* (*selective, passive*), *-able* or *-ible* (*capable, visible*), *-al* (*local, partial*), *-ar* (*insular, polar*), *-ic* (*electric, eccentric*), *-id* (*liquid, timid*) and *-ous* (*viscous, various*). Formally irregular are the relatively few nouns in *-ity* formed from adjectives outside this range, e.g. *dense, immense, pure, rare*. (Compare *dense* with *tense*: they look alike, but they form their abstract nouns *density* and *tension* in different ways.) Also somewhat capricious is the behaviour of adjectives in *-ous*, some of which preserve this suffix in the allomorph *-os-*, e.g. *viscosity, curiosity*, while others lose it, e.g. *ferocity, variety* related to *ferocious, various* – an idiosyncrasy already noted in Section 5.5. By contrast, *-th* is formally quite irregular, in that the adjectives that choose it share no common structural characteristic beyond the fact that they are monosyllabic (*deep, wide, broad, long, strong*) – a characteristic that they share with hundreds of other adjectives, however.

The behaviour of -*ness* and -*ity* shows that regularity does not imply generality. Even with the bases where -*ity* is regular, it is by no means totally general. It is easy to think of adjectives which on formal grounds are suitable bases for a noun in -*ity* but for which no such corresponding noun is in common use. Examples are *offensive, aggressive, social, chemical, lunar, nuclear, strategic, allergic, languid, horrid, gracious, devious.* I say 'not in common use' rather than 'never used', because a noun such as *offensivity, sociality* or *languidity* does not sound wrong in the way that **richity* or **greenth* does. A check in a large dictionary may reveal that some of these nouns have indeed been used. The important point, however, is that a noun in -*ity* does not exist automatically just through the existence of a suitable base adjective, as with *dioeciousness* and *dioecious*. The suffix -*ity* has more gaps in its distribution, even in the domain where it is regular, than the suffix -*ness* has. This kind of gappiness is particularly characteristic of suffixes borrowed directly or indirectly from Latin, rather than inherited from Proto-Germanic – a topic to which we return in Chapter 9.

The kinds of formal regularity that we have discussed so far have involved characteristics of the base that are either purely syntactic (for example, the bases to which -*ness* attaches are adjectives) or partly morphological (for example, the bases to which -*ity* attaches are adjectives that contain certain suffixes). But formal regularity can involve phonology too. The noun-forming suffix -*al*, illustrated at (17) in Chapter 5, can be attached only to bases whose final syllable is stressed. Thus the actual nouns *survival, proposal, referral* and *committal* are all formally regular, but the hypothetical nouns **edital, *punishal* and **reckonal* are non-existent not merely by accident but because they are formally irregular, violating the final-stress requirement. (Only one noun exists that violates this requirement, namely *burial*.) Does it follow, then, that any verb with final stress can be the base for a noun in -*al*? This question recalls a topic touched on in Chapter 5, namely the phonological requirement that verb-forming suffix -*en* can attach only to monosyllabic bases that end in plosives (as in *redden, thicken, dampen*) or fricatives (as in *stiffen, lengthen*). In Chapter 5 we left unanswered the question whether all such adjectives are bases for existing verbs with -*en*, or whether there are hypothetical verbs that do not exist even though they comply with the phonological requirement. It is in fact quite easy to find relevant examples. The verb meaning 'make wet' that corresponds to the adjective *wet* is not '*wetten*', as one might expect, but simply *wet*; and there is no '*limpen*' corresponding to *limp* (meaning 'flabby'), nor '*badden*' corresponding to *bad*. Similarly, despite the existence of *reversal* based on *reverse*, there is no '*conversal*' based on *converse*; and, despite the existence of *arrival, revival* and *survival,* there is no '*derival*' based on *derive.* So -*al* suffixation and -*en* suffixation, although they both exhibit formal regularity of a phonological kind, are both less than totally general.

If a derivational process can be formally regular without being highly general, it is natural to ask whether the reverse situation can obtain: can a process be general without being formally regular? This would be the situation of a process that is used in the formation of relatively many lexemes, but so randomly that one cannot discern any formal or structural characteristics shared by the bases that undergo it. Imagine, for example, that the adverb-forming -*ly* suffix could be attached not only to adjectives but also to nouns and verbs, so as to form numerous adverbs such as '*invently*' (meaning 'inventively') and '*gloomly*' (meaning 'gloomily') – but that the existence of such noun-derived and verb-derived adverbs (as well as of adjective-derived ones) is haphazard and unpredictable, so there happens to exist no word '*selectly*' (meaning 'selectively'), nor '*cheerly*' (meaning 'cheerily'). It is hard to find any example in English of a derivational process so haphazard as that. But this is not surprising, because it is hard to imagine how a collection of words with just these properties would come into existence. Unless a process is relatively regular, few new words are likely to be created by means of it, or to become established in general usage once they have been introduced – so, if -*ly* suffixation were as irregular as we are assuming, the class of words exhibiting it would never be likely to be numerous. We can therefore take it that in practice, although not by definition, formal generality presupposes formal regularity, but not vice versa.

8.3 Productivity in meaning: semantic regularity

A derivational process is **semantically regular** if the contribution that it makes to the meaning of the lexemes produced by it is uniform and consistent. An example is adverb-forming -*ly*. This is not only formally regular (like -*ness*) but also semantically regular, in that it almost always contributes the meaning 'in an X fashion' or 'to an X degree'. Semantic and formal regularity can diverge, however. Again, the suffix -*ity* provides handy illustration. As we have seen, -*ity* nouns are formally regular when derived from adjectives with a range of suffixes such as -*ive*, -*al* and -*ar*, and the nouns *selectivity, locality, partiality* and *polarity* all exist. It may strike you, however, that none of these nouns means exactly what one might expect on the basis of the meaning of the base adjective. *Selectivity* has a technical meaning related to radio reception, not shared with *selectiveness*, which has only the expected non-technical meaning. The adjective *local* can mean 'confined to small areas', but *locality* means never 'confinement to small areas' but always 'neighbourhood'. The noun *partiality* can mean either 'incompleteness' or 'favourable bias', just as *partial* can mean either 'incomplete' or 'biased'; however, the noun more often has the second meaning while the adjective more often has the first. And one can use the noun *polarity* in talking about electric current, but not in talking about the climate in Antarctica.

Similar behaviour is exhibited by the adjective-forming suffix *-able*. This is formally regular and general; the bases to which it can attach are transitive verbs, and there is scarcely any transitive verb for which a corresponding adjective in *-able* is idiosyncratically lacking, including a brand-new verb such as *de-Yeltsinise*. However, Exercise 1 of Chapter 2 has already drawn attention to the fact that *-able* adjectives can exhibit semantic irregularity, as *readable* and *punishable* do. In the same exercise, too, we noted that words formed with the suffix *-ion* and even some words with the formally highly regular *-ly* and *-ness* are not entirely predictable in meaning.

This divergence between formal and semantic regularity in derivation contrasts sharply with how inflection behaves, as described in Chapter 4. There, semantic regularity is the norm even where formal processes differ, for example, no past tense form of a verb has any unexpected extra meaning or function, whether it is formally regular (e.g. *performed*) or irregular (e.g. *brought, sang*). This contrast is not so surprising, however, if one remembers that word forms related by inflection are all forms of one lexeme, and therefore necessarily belong to one lexical item, whereas word forms related by derivation belong to different lexemes and therefore, at least potentially, different lexical items. Although, as we saw in Chapter 2, a lexeme does not necessarily have to be listed in a dictionary, lexemes have a kind of independence from one another that allows them to drift apart semantically, even though it does not require it.

Another illustration of how semantic and formal regularity can diverge is supplied by verbs with the bound root *-mit*. In Chapter 5 we noted that the three nouns *commitment*, *committal* and *commission* all have meanings related to meanings of the verb *commit*, but the distribution of these meanings among the three nouns is not predictable in a way that would allow an adult learner of English to guess it. Also, there is no way that a learner could guess that *commission* can also mean 'payment to a salesperson for achieving a sale', because this is not obviously related to any meaning of the verb. It follows that the suffixation of *-ion* is by no means perfectly regular semantically. But consider its formal status, by comparison with other noun-forming suffixes, as shown in (1):

(1)

	-ion	-al	-ment	-ance	*stress shift*
admit	✓			✓	
commit	✓	✓	✓		
permit	✓				✓
remit	✓	?		✓	✓
transmit	✓	?		?	

(The question marks indicate words which are not in my active vocabulary but which I would not be surprised to hear; indeed, *transmittance* exists as a technical term in physics, meaning 'measure of the ability to transmit radiation'.) The pattern of ticks, question marks and gaps seems random – except for the consistent ticks in the -*ion* column. It seems that -*ion* suffixation is formally regular with the root -*mit*; that is, for any verb with the root -*mit*, there is guaranteed to be a corresponding abstract noun in -*mission*. That being so, it seems natural to expect that the meanings of these nouns should be entirely regular. Yet we have already seen that for *commission* this is not so. *Remission*, too, is semantically irregular, in that the meanings of *remit* and -*ion* are not sufficient to determine the sense 'temporary improvement during a progressive illness'. So the fact that a noun in -*mission* is guaranteed to exist for every verb in -*mit* does not mean that, for any individual such noun, a speaker who encounters it for the first time will be able to predict confidently what it means.

The converse of the situation just described would be one in which a number of different lexemes (not just inflectional forms of lexemes) exhibit a regular pattern of semantic relationship, but without any formally regular derivational processes accompanying it. Such a situation exists with some nouns that classify domestic animals according to sex and age:

(2)

Species		horse	pig	cow	sheep	goose
Adult:	*Male*	stallion	boar	bull	ram	gander
	Female	mare	sow	cow	ewe	goose
Young		foal	piglet	calf	lamb	gosling

Not many areas of vocabulary have such a tight semantic structure as this. However, the existence of just a few such areas shows that reasonably complex patterns of semantic relationship can sustain themselves without morphological underpinning. Morphology may help in expressing such relationships (as with *pig* and *piglet*, *goose* and *gosling*), but it is not essential. This reinforces further the need to distinguish between two aspects of 'productivity': formal and semantic regularity.

8.4 Semantic blocking

The pattern of semantic relationships exhibited at (2) illustrates a further point about the way in which meaning interacts with derivation. Why are there no words such as 'cowlet' and 'sheepling', formed with the same suffixes as *piglet* and *gosling*, and with corresponding meanings? Intuitively, one feels that it has something to do with the fact that the words *calf* and *lamb* exist, with exactly the meanings that 'cowlet' and 'sheepling' would have. But that would work as an explanation only if the existence of exact synonyms is, for some reason, not tolerated or at least discouraged. Is there any evidence for that?

At first sight, pairs of exact synonyms are easy to find: *courgettes* and *zucchini*, for example, or *despise* and *scorn*, or *nearly* and *almost*. But on closer examination one finds either that the words in each pair belong to different dialects, or that they are not after all completely interchangeable. Thus, *zucchini* is used in the USA while *courgettes* is more general in Britain; *Bill scorned our apology* implies that Bill rejected it, whereas *Bill despised our apology* means rather that he despised us for offering it; and one cannot substitute *almost* for *nearly* in the phrase *not nearly* meaning 'far from', as in *I'm not nearly ready yet.* What's more, from research into the acquisition of vocabulary in early childhood, we know that children assume that every new word means something new, and is not merely an alternative for a word already learned. So our intuition that *calf* and *lamb* somehow 'block' 'cowlet' and 'sheepling' is supported by evidence. Let us define **semantic blocking** as the phenomenon whereby the existence of a word (whether simple or derived) with a particular meaning inhibits the morphological derivation, even by formally regular means, of another word with precisely that meaning.

For a nice illustration of the operation of semantic blocking, consider the nouns corresponding to the adjectives *curious* and *glorious*. The suffix *-ous* yields a formally regular base for the suffixation of *-ity*, so we might expect the corresponding nouns to be *curiosity* and 'gloriosity'. In fact, *curiosity* is in regular use but 'gloriosity' is not. The reason is that 'gloriosity' is blocked semantically by the noun *glory*, which (so to speak) pre-empts the relevant meaning. On the other hand, there is no noun such as 'cury' that might block the derivation of *curiosity* from *curious*.

For a further illustration, consider a set of nouns that correspond to verbs expressing emotional attitude:

(3) like   liking
    dislike   dislike
    love   love
    hate   hatred
    admire   admiration

The nouns are formed in a variety of ways, including conversion, but semantically they are regular. What of the verb *despise*, however? We might expect to find a suffixally derived noun to correspond to it, such as '*despisement*' or '*despisal*'. But these are blocked by the noun *contempt*, which stands in the same semantic relationship to *despise* as *admiration* does to *admire*. The relationship between *despise* and *contempt* looks rather like the relationship in inflectional morphology between *go* and *went*, which we called 'suppletive'. However, there is an important difference: *go* and *went* are morphologically related, despite their lack of a shared root, in that they are forms of the same lexeme, like *organise* and *organised*; on the other hand, *despise* and *contempt* belong to different lexemes, so their lack of a shared root means that there is no morphological relationship between them at all, except indirectly through blocking. The same sort of reason can plausibly be invoked to explain why an adjective such as '*ungood*' does not exist, as noted in Chapter 5, even though *un-* is formally and semantically so general: it is blocked by *bad*, with which it would be exactly synonymous, just as '*unlong*' would be synonymous with *short*, '*unhot*' with *cold*, and so on.

According to the definition of semantic blocking, even a formally regular process can be blocked. As an illustration, consider the formation of adverbs in *-ly* from adjectives, as in *quickly* and *slowly*. This a formally regular and general process; even so, the idiosyncratic existence of an adverb without *-ly* may block it, as with the adjective *fast*, whose corresponding adverb is simply *fast*, not '*fastly*'. Likewise, the semantically regular abstract noun corresponding to *high* is *height*, which blocks the use of *highness* in this sense. However, *highness* (unlike '*fastly*') exists because it has acquired a technical metaphorical sense in expressions such as *Your Royal Highness*.

In inflectional morphology, the blocking effect of suppletion is absolute. The existence of *went* means that *goed will never be used, unless by a young child or an adult learner. Derivational morphology, however, is less tightly structured than inflectional, so semantic blocking can be a matter of degree. Just as formally regular '*longness*' seems less odd than irregular *greyth, so *gloriousness* with its highly general suffix sounds more natural than '*gloriosity*' with its less general one. The blocking effect of *glory* has to compete with the regularity and generality of *-ness* suffixation, and may not always win. Even so, if we encounter *gloriousness*, we expect its use to be differentiated, even if only minimally, from that of *glory*.

8.5 Productivity in compounding

In Chapter 6, we noted that much the most common kind of compound in English is the compound noun, whether primary (e.g. *hairnet*) or secondary (e.g. *hair restorer*). It is on compound nouns of the NN type that I will concentrate here. It turns out that primary and secondary compounds are both highly regular formally, but only secondary compounds are highly regular semantically. Again, therefore, the distinction between formal and semantic regularity turns out to be useful.

As we noted in Chapter 6, the most natural way to interpret *hair restorer* is 'substance for restoring hair growth'; that is, to interpret the first component (*hair*) as the object of the verbal element in the second (*restore*). A secondary compound for which this mode of interpretation yields the right meaning is semantically regular, therefore. All the secondary compounds given at (17) in Chapter 6, namely *sign-writer*, *slum clearance*, *crime prevention*, *wish-fulfilment*, are semantically regular. But there exist also semantically irregular compounds with the appearance of secondary compounds:

(4) machine-washing, globe-trotter, voice-activation

Machine-washing may in some context be interpreted 'washing of machines', but more often it means washing in a washing-machine, as opposed to by hand. A globe-trotter is someone who travels around the world a lot, not someone who 'trots globes' (whatever that would mean). In voice-activation, it is not a voice that is activated but rather a machine (say, a computer) that is activated by spoken commands rather than by a keyboard or mouse.

There is room for debate whether these are secondary compounds of a semantically unusual kind, or primary compounds in which the second component just happens to be derived from a verb. How is it most useful to define the term 'secondary compound': more narrowly, so that the first component must be the object of the verbal element, or more widely, so as to permit the first component to be related to the verbal element in some other way, for example as instrument (*machine-washing*) or location (*globe-trotter*)? It is not important to give a firm answer to that question here. What one can say, however, is that the semantic unpredictability of the examples at (4) is far from unusual among NN compounds; in fact, it is a kind of unpredictability shared by all primary compounds. Recall from Chapter 6 the discussion of *hairnet, mosquito net* and *butterfly net*. It is not the structure of these compounds, in conjunction with the meanings of the components, that tells us precisely what each stands for; rather, it is our knowledge of the world, such as the difference in the ways that mosquitos and butterflies impinge on human beings. Primary NN compounds are thus intrinsically irregular semantically, in that their exact interpretation is unpredictable without the help of this sort of real-world knowledge.

The semantic irregularity of primary compounds does not entail any formal irregularity, however. In fact, any two nouns whatever can be juxtaposed in English to produce a formally acceptable root compound. For example, *bóat moon* and *brídge cloud*, with stress on the first element as indicated, are possible English nouns even though neither has ever been used (so far as I know) and it is not clear what either of them would mean except in the vaguest terms ('moon associated somehow with boats' and 'cloud associated somehow with bridges'). This semantic vagueness may seem to present an intolerable obstacle to the creation of new root compounds. However, the obstacle is smaller than it may at first seem, for two reasons. Firstly, the elements in a new root compound XY may be such that even the vague interpretation 'Y somehow associated with X' is precise enough for practical purposes. For example, consider the elaborate compound word in (5), which might conceivably figure in a newspaper headline:

(5)

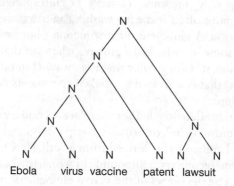

The fact that a reader has never encountered this compound before is no barrier to understanding it, just on the strength of general knowledge about the patentability of drugs. Secondly, even in more obscure cases, we instinctively grasp at contextual clues to fill in semantic gaps. I will illustrate this with an actual example.

It is unlikely that any readers have previously encountered the compound *cup bid float*, and unlikely too that many readers, having now encountered it, will be able to hazard much of a guess as to its meaning. Yet it is a word that actually appeared in the *The Press* newspaper in

Christchurch, New Zealand, on 14 April 1994. *The Press* had a column on the front page summarising the main stories on inside pages. *Cup bid float* appeared as the headline for one of these summaries, which continued: 'New Zealanders will be offered the chance to buy shares in the company that will finance yachtsman Chris Dickson's bid to win the America's Cup next year.' With just that much contextual information, the interpretation of the enigmatic headline becomes clear. *Cup* denotes the America's Cup, *cup bid* denotes an attempt to win it (*bid* being an alternative to *attempt* that is favoured in newspaper headlines for the sake of brevity), and *float* refers to the floating of a limited company, i.e. the offer of shares in it on the share market. The fact that the headline cannot be interpreted without the help of the paragraph that it introduces hardly matters, from the journalist's point of view; it has served its purpose if it has persuaded readers to read on.

English makes more generous use of compounding than many other European languages do, so it is hardly surprising that at least some kinds of compounding should be formally regular and also highly general. What is more surprising is that such a general process should be so vague semantically. Interpretation of new compounds relies in practice less on strictly linguistic regularities than on context and general knowledge.

8.6 Measuring productivity: the significance of neologisms

So far, I have discussed various aspects of the productivity of derivational processes, such as *-ity* and *-ness* suffixation, without the help of any objectively quantifiable measurements. I have not introduced any scale from 0 to 1, say, in terms of which *-ness* might score 0.9 and *-ity* 0.5. This may look like a serious defect. Any conclusions about formal regularity and generality, in particular, must be more or less subjective unless they are based on figures, one may think. What we need is a comparison between the actual frequency of a process and its potential frequency, appropriately defined. The more closely the 'actual' figure approaches the 'potential' figure, the more productive the process is, in some sense.

In practice, however, devising such a measure has turned out to be extremely tricky. For example, I suggested earlier that *-ity* is formally regular when applied to adjectives with certain suffixes such as *-ous*, *-ive* and *-able*, but otherwise irregular, for example, when it is attached to suffixless adjectives. This has the advantage that a non-existent noun such as 'richity' can be classed as formally irregular, but the disadvantage that it entails that actual nouns such as *purity*, *sanity*, *oddity* and *severity* must be irregular too. If we dislike this outcome, we must extend the range of adjectives that count as potential bases for *-ity* suffixation so as to include at least *pure, sane, odd* and *severe*. But how far should this extension go? If the new potential bases are taken to be just those un-suffixed adjectives for which corresponding nouns in *-ity* exist, then the ratio of actual to potential *-ity* nouns will remain high – but only because we have contrived that it should be so. If, at the other extreme, we let *pure, sane, odd* and *severe* persuade us that any adjective whatever can be a potential base, then the actual-to-potential ratio dwindles to almost zero, and our measure fails to capture the difference in 'feel' between '*gloriosity*' (plausible, but blocked by *glory*) and **richity* (highly implaus-ible). What is the appropriate intermediate position between these extremes, then? It is hard to answer that question except subjectively. Thus the objectivity that a numerical ratio would supply turns out to be frustratingly elusive.

Since about 1990, however, a new set of numerical measures have been devised that avoid subjective bias and yet seem to correspond well to what we feel we mean when we talk about 'productivity'. These measures exploit the extremely large corpora, or bodies of linguistic material, that have been assembled on computer by linguists and dictionary-makers for the purpose of studying both the frequency with which words (lexemes and word forms) occur and the contexts in which they occur. For a process to be productive, in one sense, it should be a process that can be used to form brand new lexemes, or **neologisms**. So can we identify neologisms in one of these large corpora? Unfortunately, we cannot do so directly; all we can tell for certain is that a lexeme with an earlier dated occurrence in the corpus is not brand new. However, we can rely on the fact that most neologisms within the corpus will be rare. In fact, all will be rare except those that quickly become fashionable. So, even if we cannot directly identify neologisms, an alternative that is both appropriate and feasible is to identify words that are extremely rare, especially those that appear only once in the whole corpus: so-called **hapax legomena** (singular **hapax legomenon**), a Greek expression borrowed from classical studies, meaning 'said (only) once'. We can now focus on the morphological processes that are used in hapax legomena (and other very rare words), and compare them with processes that are used in more frequently occurring words.

Such studies shed interesting new light on the relationship between the familar pair *-ity* and *-ness*. In the Cobuild corpus of about eighteen million English word-tokens (based at Birmingham University and used by the dictionary publisher Collins), the number of word-types exhibit-ing *-ity* (roughly 400) is not greatly less than the number exhibiting *-ness* (roughly 500). However, most of the *-ity* words are of common occur-rence (more technically, their token-frequency is high), while many more of the types exhibiting -*ness* have low token frequency, including hapax legomena. That is, although by one measure -*ness* seems to be not much more productive than -*ity* is, it is far more likely than -*ity* to be used in the creation of neologisms.

The suffix -*ness* rates high both in the number of words that contain it (words as types, that is, not tokens), and in its availability for neologisms. The suffix -*ity* ranks high by the first measure but low by the second. Could an affix rank low by the first measure and high by the second? The answer is yes. The Cobuild corpus contains relatively few word-types with the suffix -*ian* (as in *Canadian, Wagnerian*), yet a very high proportion of these are of low token-frequency. Rather surprisingly, therefore, for an affix to be suitable for use in a brand new word, it does not have to appear in a large number of existing words.

There is far more that could be said about the ways in which studies of very large corpora can shed light on word formation in English. To understand it in greater depth presupposes some knowledge of statistical techniques, however. For present purposes, it is enough to be aware that such statistical studies are being carried out, and that they go a considerable way towards firming up the notions of generality and formal regularity which I defined in an unquantified fashion earlier in the chapter.

8.7 Conclusion: 'productivity' in syntax

I hope to have made it clear both why productivity is a notion that must be approached cautiously, and how it is possible to untangle its various aspects. The most important findings to bear in mind are two. First, a process can be formally regular without being semantically regular, as is illustrated by the suffixation of -*ion* to produce nouns from verbs with the root -*mit*. Secondly, semantically regular relationships between lexemes (that is semantic relationships that have more or less widespread parallels involving other lexemes) can subsist without morphological support, as is illustrated by the terms for domestic animals at (2). If semantic and formal regularity often go together, that is hardly surprising, since lexemes so constructed will be relatively easy to learn and will provide the most natural models on which new lexemes can be created; but it is oversimplifying to classify as simply 'irregular' or 'unproductive' any morphological relationship that is not in all respects straightforward.

It is natural to ask why productivity crops up as an issue so insistently with word formation but not with sentence formation. Are there no syntactic constructions that are less productive than others? Such constructions do indeed seem to exist. For example, there is no obvious reason why the construction illustrated at (6), in which a verb has two objects, should be acceptable in those examples but unacceptable (or less readily acceptable) in the examples at (7):

(6) a. They gave us a present.
    b. They faxed us the answer.
    c. They allocated us two seats.
    d. They baked us a cake.

(7) a. *They donated us some pictures.
    b. *They yelled us the instructions.
    c. *They planned us a holiday.
    d. *They spoiled us the evening.

Seemingly, the lexical entries for at least some of these verbs must specify whether or not they tolerate the double-object construction. The reason why this sort of syntactic restriction is less usual than the kind of morphological restriction discussed in this chapter is not immediately obvious. It may simply be that the propensity for words (i.e. lexemes) to become lexical items, and thus to acquire idiosyncrasies, inevitably compromises the generality of the processes whereby complex words are formed (that is, processes of derivational morphology and compounding); on the other hand, the propensity for phrases to become lexical items is relatively weak. But why should this difference in propensity for lexical listing exist, given that (as Chapter 2 showed) wordhood is neither a necessary nor a sufficient condition for lexical-item status? A plausible answer is that shorter items are more likely to be lexically listed than longer items are, and words (even complex words) are generally shorter than phrases.

Exercises

1. Consider the following verbs with the bound root *-fer*: *confer, defer, infer, prefer, refer, transfer.* Make a chart showing which existing nouns are derived from them by means of the suffixes *-ment, -al* and *-ence* and by stress shift (compare the verb *permít* and the noun *pérmit*). What relationship (if any) between formal and semantic regularity emerges?

2. The commonest way of forming the past tense of English verbs is by suffixing *-ed* (see Chapter 4). It does not follow that this is formally the most regular process for all verbs, without exception. Consider the verbs whose basic form rhymes with *find: bind, blind, find, mind, remind, wind,* and any others you can think of. Is there any evidence that, for these verbs

in particular, another process may be formally more regular than suffixation of -ed?

3. For each verb or verb phrase (X) in the following list, give (i) the word
you would most probably use to mean 'someone who Xs habitually or as
an occupation' and (ii) the meaning of the noun of the form Xer. How do
these examples illustrate the relationship between formal regularity,
semantic blocking, and semantic regularity?

(a)	*sing*	(e)	*spy*
(b)	*cook*	(f)	*clean*
(c)	*steal*	(g)	*pray*
(d)	*cycle*	(h)	*play the flute*

4. Compare in respect of formal and semantic regularity the suffix -*ish*
when used in forming adjectives from adjectives (e.g. *greenish*) and when
used in forming adjectives from nouns (e.g. *boyish*).

Recommendations for reading

Many writers on morphology try to draw a hard-and-fast distinction
between 'productive' and 'unproductive' processes, and then announce
that they are concerned only with 'productive' ones. The more nuanced
approach that I have adopted owes a large debt to Corbin (1987),
summarised in Carstairs-McCarthy (1992).

The phenomenon of semantic blocking has been discussed since
the nineteenth century. Among recent linguistic theorists, interest in it
was revived by Aronoff (1976). Clark (1993) discusses the evidence that
young children's acquisition of new vocabulary is assisted by an implicit
assumption that no new word has exactly the same meaning as a word
they already know.

An early approach to quantifying degrees of productivity is that of
Jackendoff (1975). The study of hapax legomena in large corpora, as a
measure of one kind of productivity, was pioneered by Baayen (1992).
For further discussion, see subsequent issues of *Yearbook of Morphology*.
On the relationship between lexical listedness and length, see Di Sciullo
and Williams (1987).

9 The historical sources of English word formation

9.1 Introduction

This chapter does not attempt to summarise the whole history of the English language. Instead, I will concentrate on just those aspects of its history over the past thousand years or so that help to account for some of the peculiarities of word formation in contemporary English. In derivational morphology, history sheds light in particular on the distribution of free and bound roots, discussed in Chapter 3, and on the differences in 'productivity' (especially as regards neologisms) that we observed in Chapter 8. In inflectional morphology, what is striking is the transformation of English from a language with elaborate inflectional morphology (some individual lexemes having a dozen or more forms) to one in which inflection plays a much more limited role.

9.2 Germanic, Romance and Greek vocabulary

English is a West Germanic language, related closely to the other West Germanic languages (Dutch, German, Frisian and Afrikaans) and less closely to the North Germanic languages (Norwegian, Danish, Swedish, Icelandic and Faeroese). On the other hand, England was ruled for a long period after 1066 by a monarch and a nobility whose native language was a variety of French; and even though this ruling group gradually switched to English for everyday purposes, French remained in use much longer as a language of law and administration, and longer still as a language of culture that every educated person was expected to learn. It is not surprising, then, that the vocabulary of English contains a high proportion of words borrowed from French – a much higher proportion than in the other Germanic languages.

French is one of the so-called Romance languages, descended from Latin, along with Portuguese, Spanish, Catalan, Provençal, Romansh (spoken in Switzerland), Italian (with its many diverse dialects), and

Romanian. Most words borrowed from French therefore come from Latin indirectly. But Latin has had a more direct influence too. Three thousand years ago it was spoken only in a small area around Rome, but by AD 400 it was the official language of the western half of the Roman Empire and the vehicle of a huge and varied written literature, second only to Greek and far outweighing in scope and variety any other written literature in Europe until well after the invention of printing. It was also the liturgical language of all West European Christians until the Protestant Reformation of the sixteenth century, and remained the predominant liturgical language of Catholics worldwide until the 1970s. As a language of scholarly publication, it survived in use until the eighteenth century (for example, Sir Isaac Newton published in Latin his work on physics and astronomy). The study of Latin was still a routine part of what was considered a 'good education' throughout the English-speaking world until the second half of the twentieth century. So, particularly after the Renaissance, or revival of learning, in the fifteenth and sixteenth centuries, it is not surprising that many words were adopted into English from Latin directly, rather than by way of French.

The Romans revered Greek culture, and most of classical Latin literature emulates Greek models. However, the Latin of classical (pre-Christian) literature did not use many Greek words, the Romans preferring instead to create new Latin terms to translate Greek ones. Latin borrowings from Greek increased after the adoption of Christianity as the state religion of the Empire in the fourth century. The possibility of direct Greek influence on English did not arise, however, until Western Europeans began to learn about Greek culture for themselves in the fifteenth century. (This revival of interest was stimulated partly by a westward migration of Greek scholars from Constantinople, later called Istanbul, after it was captured by the Ottoman Turks in 1453.) From the point of view of word formation, the main influence of Greek has been in its use in the invention of scientific and technical words, and many of the bound combining forms discussed in Chapter 6 are Greek in origin.

The variety of the sources that have contributed to the vocabulary of English accounts for the existence of many pairs or groups of words that are descended, in whole or in part, from the same ancestral morpheme in the extinct Proto-Indo-European language from which Greek and the Romance and Germanic languages are descended – words that are thus **cognate**, in the terminology of historical linguistics – but that have reached their contemporary English form by a variety of routes, through direct inheritance or through borrowing at different times. An example is the Proto-Indo-European root from which the English word *heart* is descended. Regular sound changes have affected this root in all those languages that preserve it, so in Latin it shows up as *cord-* (a bound root, as the hyphen indicates). In French this becomes *cœur*, from which was formed a derivative *courage*, with a metaphorical meaning ('heart, disposition'). *Courage* was borrowed into English around 1300, and is attested with its modern sense in 1375. However, around 1400 the same root was borrowed again, in its Latin shape, in the word *cordial*, with the meaning 'belonging to the heart' and later 'warm, friendly'. Yet a fourth version of this root appears in *cardiac*, borrowed around 1600 from the Greek word *kardiakós* 'pertaining to the heart', which displays the root in its Greek guise *kard-*.

Another Indo-European root that has reached modern English vocabulary through three distinct sources of borrowing as well as by direct inheritance is the root from which the verb *bear* is derived. This shows up in Latin as *fer-* and in Greek as *pher-*, both meaning 'carry'. These appear in modern English, the former as the bound root in verbs such as *confer*, and latter in the name *Christopher*, which originates in the legend of a saint who carried Christ across a river. But English has also acquired the root via French, in *suffer*, corresponding to modern French *souffrir*. (The difference in stress between *confer* and *suffer* is a clue that one has reached English via a 'learned' route, directly from Latin, while the other has come via medieval spoken French.)

A striking feature of these words is that the inherited Germanic forms, *heart* and *bear*, are free, whereas in the forms borrowed from Latin, French or Greek the cognate roots are bound. This highlights an important morphological difference between inherited and borrowed words. In borrowing these words, English speakers borrowed not only the roots and affixes that they contain but also the pattern of word formation that they conform to – a pattern which does not allow roots to appear naked, so to speak, unaccompanied by some derivational or inflectional affix. Admittedly, some borrowed roots are free, and a few inherited ones are bound. It is still true, however, that most of the roots that are bound in all contexts (that is, most of the roots that have no free allomorphs) do not belong to the vocabulary that English has inherited from its Proto-Germanic ancestor.

9.3 The rarity of borrowed inflectional morphology

One way in which a root can avoid appearing naked is if it is accompanied by an inflectional affix. At first sight, then, it may seem that, if English borrows a foreign pattern of word formation, it should be expected to borrow inflectional affixes that conform to that pattern, as well as roots and derivational affixes. In fact, this scarcely happens;

English does not use French or Latin inflectional affixes on verbs borrowed from those languages, for example. However, this is not so surprising when one bears in mind that the new items that a language acquires through borrowing are lexemes rather than individual word forms, for reasons that I will explain.

If English speakers import a new verb V from French, they will not import just its past tense form (say), since (as explained in Chapter 4) we expect to be able to express in English not only the grammatical word 'past tense of V' but also the grammatical words 'third person singular present of V', 'perfect participle of V', and so on. But it is not convenient for English speakers to pick these word forms out of the repertoire of forms that V has in French, partly because that presupposes a knowledge of French grammar, and partly because there may be no French grammatical word exactly corresponding to 'third person singular present', 'perfect participle', and so on. It is much more convenient to equip the new French-sourced verb with word forms created in accordance with English verbal inflection – specifically, the most regular pattern of verbal inflection (suffixes -s, -ed and -ing). And that is precisely what happens.

The only condition under which English speakers are likely to borrow foreign word forms along with the lexemes that they belong to is if the grammatical words that the word forms express are few in number (and thus not hard to learn), and if their functions in English and the source language correspond closely. This condition is fulfilled with nouns. English nouns have only two forms, singular and plural; and, if a noun is borrowed from a source language that also distinguishes singular and plural inflectionally, then the foreign inflected plural form may be borrowed too. Here are some examples involving Latin, Greek and Hebrew, which resemble English in distinguishing singular and plural forms in nouns:

(1) | Source language | Singular | Plural |
|---|---|---|
| Greek | phenomenon | phenomena |
| | schema | schemata |
| Latin | cactus | cacti |
| | formula | formulae |
| | datum | data |
| Hebrew | cherub | cherubim |
| | kibbutz | kibbutzim |

These foreign plurals are all vulnerable, however. *Phenomena* and *data* seem solidly established, but for the others it is probably more usual now to hear or read *schemas, cactuses, formulas, cherubs* and *kibbutzes*. Even *data* tends to be accommodated to English morphology, but by a different method: many speakers treat it not as plural (*these data are* ...) but as singular (*this data is* ...), and the corresponding singular form *datum* tends to be replaced by *piece of data* (rather like *piece of toast* in relation to *toast*).

(You may wonder why I have not mentioned French as a source for borrowed plural inflection, given the importance of the French component in English vocabulary. The reason is that the usual plural suffix in both medieval and modern French is -*s*, just as in English. A plural word form borrowed from French would therefore nearly always be indistinguishable from one inflected in the regular English fashion. Just a few French borrowings sometimes retain, in formal written English, an idiosyncratic plural suffix -*x*, e.g. *tableaux, plateaux*.)

The effect of these borrowings is to divide the class of nouns with irregular plurals (i.e. plurals not involving -*s*) into two classes: nouns that belong to everyday vocabulary and whose irregular plural survives because it is in reasonably frequent use (e.g. *teeth, children, mice*), and relatively rare or technical nouns whose irregular plural survives (if at all) as a badge of learning or sophistication. What we do not find are irregular plurals that fall between these extremes, in nouns that are not particularly common but do not belong to technical or learned vocabulary either. (At first sight, an example of this kind may seem to be *oxen*, the plural of the noun *ox*; but, in English-speaking countries where the dominant religion is Christianity, this unusual plural form is almost certainly kept alive by its occurrence in the Gospel Nativity story.)

9.4 The reduction in inflectional morphology

In Chapter 4 we noted that modern English nouns have no more than two inflected word forms: singular and plural. In Old English, however, there was superimposed on this number contrast a contrast of case, like that found in modern English personal pronouns (nominative *we* versus accusative *us* etc.), but more extensive: Old English nouns could distinguish also a genitive (or possessive) case, and a dative case whose meanings included that of modern *to* in *Mary gave the book to John*. These two numbers and four cases yielded a pattern of eight grammatical words for each noun lexeme, as illustrated at (2) and (3):

(2)

	Singular	Plural
Nominative	nama 'name'	naman
Accusative	naman	naman
Genitive	naman	namena
Dative	naman	namum

(3)

	Singular	Plural
Nominative	stān 'stone'	stānas
Accusative	stān	stānas
Genitive	stānes	stāna
Dative	stāne	stānum

As will be seen, neither NAMA nor STĀN had eight distinct word forms, one for each grammatical word; instead, they display different patterns of syncretism. However, all Old English nouns had more than the meager two forms that are available in modern English.

If nouns distinguished four cases in Old English, it is reasonable to guess that pronouns should have done so too; and that guess is correct. (In fact Old English pronouns sometimes had five cases, including an instrumental.) What is more, the same two numbers and four cases were available for adjectives and determiners (counterparts of words such as that and this), along with a distinction that has been lost in modern English: that of **gender**. As in modern German or Russian, Old English nouns were distributed among three genders (neuter, feminine and masculine), which were grammatically relevant in that they affected the inflectional affixes chosen by any adjectives and determiners that modified them. Thus, it is the distinction between masculine and feminine that accounts for the different forms of the words meaning 'the' and 'good' in se gōda fæder 'the good father' and sēo gōde mōdor 'the good mother'.

Old English verbs displayed a similar inflectional luxuriance. In Chapter 4, we noted that most modern English verbs have four distinct forms (e.g. perform, performs, performed, performing), while some common verbs have five (e.g. speak, speaks, spoke, spoken, speaking). By contrast, the typical Old English verb lexeme HELPAN 'help' had over a dozen distinct forms: a so-called 'infinitive' helpan 'to help', a perfective participle geholpen, and further forms including those whose grammatical functions are as set out in (4). (In (4), ð stands for the sound represented by th in thin, and 'indicative' and 'subjunctive' represent a contast in mood: between, very roughly, asserting a fact (e.g. John is coming) and alluding to a possibility (e.g. … that John should come in I insist that John should come).)

(4)

		Indicative	Subjunctive
	Person	Present	Present
Singular	1st ('I')	helpe	helpe
	2nd ('you')	helpest	helpe
	3rd ('(s)he')	helpeð	helpe

Plural	1st ('we')	helpaŏ	helpen
	2nd ('you')	helpaŏ	helpen
	3rd ('they')	helpaŏ	helpen

		Past	*Past*
Singular	1st	healp	hulpe
	2nd	hulpe	hulpe
	3rd	healp	hulpe
Plural	1st	hulpon	hulpen
	2nd	hulpon	hulpen
	3rd	hulpon	hulpen

Not included in (4) are the imperative forms ('help!'), or the verbal adjective *helpende*, which, just like other adjectives in Old English, had forms that distinguished three genders, two numbers and four cases.

An obvious question is: why did English lose this wealth of inflection? Like many obvious questions, this one has no straightforward answer. Partly, no doubt, the loss of inflection is due to the temporary eclipse of English by French as the language of culture and administration after 1066, and hence the weakening of the conservative influence of literacy. Partly also it is due to dialect mixture. The examples of 'Old English' that I have given here come from the dominant dialect of written literature, that of south-western England. But this was not the dialect of London, which became increasingly influential during the so-called 'Middle English' period (from about 1150 to 1500), and established itself as the main variety used in printing. For example, the spread of the noun plural suffix *-s* at the expense of its rivals is a feature of northern dialects that affected the London dialect also. English inflectional morphology was already by 1600 almost the same as in 2000, so that modern readers of Shakespeare encounter only a few obsolete inflected forms such as *thou helpest* and *he helpeth*, for *you help* and *he helps*, that preserve two Old English suffixes illustrated in (2).

9.5 Characteristics of Germanic and non-Germanic derivation

At the end of Section 9.2 it was noted that the inherited Germanic root *heart* is free while the cognate roots *cord-* and *card-*, borrowed from Latin and Greek, are bound, and the same applies to inherited *bear* by contrast with borrowed *-fer* and *-pher*. If this kind of contrast is general, then it has implications for inherited and borrowed affixes too. We will expect that native Germanic affixes should attach to free bases, while the affixes that attach to bound bases should generally be borrowed. And this turns out to be correct.

At (5) are listed most of the derivational affixes that we have considered so far, classified according to their origin:

(5) *Germanic*
   -ish
   -ed
   -en
   -er
   -hood
   -ie (*as in* doggie)
   -let
   -ship
   -y (*as in* misty)

Romance or Greek
   -((a)t)ion
   -(i)an
   -(i)fy
   -al
   -ance, -ence
   -ar
   -ent, -ant
   -ess
   -ette
   -ine
   -ise
   -ism
   -ist
   -ment
   de-
   dis-

(Some affixes not listed at (5) are left for an exercise at the end of this chapter.) It is easy to check that all the affixes in the lefthand column select exclusively or almost exclusively free bases, while most of those in the righthand column readily permit or even prefer bound ones. Compare, for example, *-let* and *-ette*, which are similar in meaning and in lack of generality: both mean roughly 'small', though neither is perfectly regular semantically, and *-ette* also sometimes means 'female'. If you are asked to list nouns formed with the suffix *-let*, you will probably think of examples such as *booklet, piglet, droplet* and *starlet*, all with clearly identifiable free bases. For nouns with the suffix *-ette*, your list is sure to include *cigarette*, and it may also include (depending on your country of origin) *suffragette, laundrette, kitchenette, maisonette* and *drum-majorette*. Among these, the bases *cigar-, laundr-* and *maison-* are bound, *cigar-* (with stress on the first syllable) and *laundr-* being bound allomorphs of *cigár* and *laundry*, and *maison-* having no free allomorph in English. So, although *-ette* is by no means restricted to bound bases, it does not avoid them in the way that *-let* does. The word *hamlet* meaning 'small village' may seem to be a counterexample. However, if, like me, you feel this to be a simple word rather than a complex one, consisting of a single morpheme rather than a root *ham-* plus *-let*, it does not count as an actual counterexample. (Historically, in fact, *hamlet* was borrowed from French, and contained originally the *-ette* suffix in a variant spelling.)

Similar conclusions emerge from comparing some abstract-noun-forming suffixes in the two columns: -*ship* and -*hood* in the Germanic column, and -*(a(t))ion*, -*ance*/-*ence*, and -*ism* in the Romance and Greek column. For the latter, it is certainly possible to find words whose bases are free (e.g. *consideration, admittance, defeatism*); however, many of the bases selected by these affixes are bound, being either bound allomorphs of roots that are elsewhere free (e.g. *consumption, preference, Catholicism*) or else roots that lack free allomorphs entirely (e.g. *condition, patience, solipsism*). In contrast, nouns in -*ship* and -*hood* always seem to have free bases: *friendship, kingship, governorship*; *childhood, adulthood, priesthood*. What we observe here is, in fact, the historical basis for a phenomenon that we noted in Chapter 3: the root of an English word is more likely to be free than bound, yet a large number of bound roots exist in modern English also, thanks to massive borrowing from French and Latin.

Describing the affixes in the second column, I was careful to say that most of them permit bound bases, not that all of them do. Some borrowed affixes associate solely or mainly with free bases, and in so doing have acquired native Germanic habits. An example at (5) is the suffix -*ment*, as in *development, punishment, commitment, attainment* – though it is sometimes found with a bound base, as in the nouns *compliment* and *supplement*. Another example is the prefix *de-*, as in *deregister, delouse* and *decompose*. This tolerance for free bases is surely connected with the fact that, in the terminology of Chapter 8, *de-* is formally and semantically rather regular, and can readily be used in neologisms (e.g. *de-grass* in *The courtyard was grassed only last year, but now they are going to de-grass it and lay paving stones*). For an affix restricted to bound bases, such a neologising capacity would be scarcely conceivable in a language where, as in English, most bases are free.

9.6 Fashions in morphology

The title of this section, like the title of Chapter 8, highlights a respect in which morphology differs from syntax. It makes sense to ask whether a certain word formation process (a particular affix, let's say) is in or out of fashion, and self-appointed language pundits comment on such changes in linguistic fashion regularly in the media. However, nobody comments on fashions in how questions are formed, or in the structure of relative clauses, for instance. Syntax is stable in a way that morphology is not. This is surely connected with the fact that, as we noted in Chapters 2 and 8, many morphological processes are haphazardly 'gappy' (that is, they may not be formally general even if they are formally and semantically regular), whereas few if any syntactic constructions are 'gappy' in this way. In morphology, gaps get filled, or else gappy processes lose their regularity and survive only in a few lexically listed lexemes, like the process of forming abstract nouns by suffixing -th to adjectives, while other processes become increasingly regular to replace them.

A systematic study of morphological fashions belongs to a historical study of English word formation rather than to an introductory survey such as this. However, I will mention two fashions that manifested themselves in the last half of the twentieth century, because both of them, in some degree, go against more general trends of the last couple of centuries. The first is a fashion for certain Latin- and Greek-derived prefixes; the second is a fashion for a certain kind of headless compound.

Conscious borrowings from Latin and (to a lesser extent) Greek were fashionable in certain literary styles of the sixteenth and seventeenth centuries, because of a perceived need to enrich the English vocabulary. But such borrowings, often obscure and even incomprehensible to ordinary readers, were also attacked as 'inkhorn terms' – mere products of the pedant's desire to show off his knowledge of Latin. The result is that the Latin- and Greek-derived element in the vocabulary of English has, since the eighteenth century, been pruned rather than increased. Histories of the English language standardly draw attention to Latin-derived words that used to be common but are no longer used, such as *eximious* 'excellent' and *demit* 'dismiss'. One might have expected, therefore, that few new words formed during the last two centuries (apart from technical terms involving combining forms) would contain Latin- or Greek-derived elements. But this is incorrect. Since the nineteenth century a small countertrend has set in, involving the Latin-derived prefixes *super-* and *sub-* and Greek-derived ones such as *hyper-*, *macro-*, *micro-* and *mega-*. Words such as *superman* (originally a translation by George Bernard Shaw of Nietzsche's German coining *Übermensch*), *superstar*, *super-rich* and *supercooling* illustrate the use with free Germanic roots of a prefix that was once typical with Latin-derived roots, often bound, as in *supersede* and *superimpose*. Words such as *hypersensitive*, *hypermarket* and *hyperactivity* (as in *attention deficit hyperactivity disorder*, or *ADHD*) illustrate a similar tendency with Greek prefix meaning 'over-, excessive(ly)', once peculiar to combining-form words such as *hypertrophy* 'excessive growth'. A more recent illustration of this trend has been the extension to free roots of Greek *mega-*, so as to create *megastore*, *mega-merger* and *megabucks* alongside earlier words such as *megalith* and *megaphone*. A contributing factor, no doubt, is a desire to show one's awareness and understanding of new technical terms incorporating *mega-*, *giga-* and *nano-*, meaning respectively 'million', '(American) billion, or thousand million', and 'one (American) billionth' (as in *nanogram* '10^{-9} grams'). Fashions in language are as hard to predict as fashions in clothing, but it will not be surprising if *giga-* and *nano-* soon acquire the same currency as *mega-*, *macro-* and *micro-*, with the meanings 'huge' and 'tiny'.

Headless or exocentric compound nouns such as *redhead*, *lazybones* and *pickpocket* do not reflect productive patterns in modern English. It would be a rash writer or speaker who coined a word such as *climbrock* or *longneck*, expecting the reader or hearer to interpret it unthinkingly as meaning 'rock climber' or 'person with a long neck'. However, there is another kind of exocentric compound noun involving a verb and an adverb or preposition, illustrated by *write-off*, *call-up*, *take-over* and *breakdown*. Usually these can be related to phrasal verbs, such as in *They wrote those debts off* and *He was called up for military service*. However, compounds do not exist corresponding to every phrasal verb; for example, I have never encountered the hypothetical nouns '*give-up*' 'surrender' or '*put-off*' 'postponement'. Even this kind of exocentric compound, therefore, seems to be only marginally productive. Yet in the 1960s there arose a vogue for a class of compounds of the form *V-in*, such as *sit-in*, *talk-in*, *love-in* and *think-in*. What is curious about these is that corresponding to most of them there is no phrasal verb. People who had participated in a twelve-hour sit-in would be unlikely to describe what they had done by saying *We sat in for twelve hours*. The phrasal-verb-based pattern of headless compound thus for a while extended its scope outside the domain where it had previously been regular (although not fully general), but with its second component restricted to the preposition *in*. This exemplifies yet again a characteristic of morphology that we discussed in Chapters 2 and 8 especially: the propensity to display random exceptions and lexical restrictions.

9.7 Conclusion: history and structure

Characteristics of a language that are due purely to historical accident are the characteristics that, in principle, are least likely to interest a general linguist. The Norman conquest in 1066 is just such an accident, so its consequences for the vocabulary of English (the massive medieval intake of words from French) may seem to deserve a place only in histories of the English language, not in books (such as this) about its morphological structure. But there is more to it than that. If it had not been for the Norman conquest and its aftermath, English morphology would not have acquired the at first sight rather bewildering mix of characteristics evident from Chapters 3 and 5. What's more, one cannot dismiss characteristics acquired through the Latin lexical intake as 'unproductive' and therefore not truly part of modern English morphology; for, as we saw in Chapter 8, some Latin-derived processes, such as suffixation of -*ion* and -*ence*, are in limited domains just as formally regular as processes such as adverb formation with -*ly*. If the history of the community of English speakers in the British Isles had been otherwise, the English language would be considerably different today not just in its repertoire of lexical items but in how its words are structured.

Exercises

Here is a set of affixes:

- (a) -*able*
- (b) -*ful* (as in the adjective *joyful*)
- (c) -*ing* (as in the noun *yearning*)
- (d) -*ity*
- (e) -*ive*
- (f) -*less* (as in the adjective *joyless*)
- (g) -*ly* (as in the adverb *happily*)
- (h) -*ly* (as in the adjective *manly*)
- (i) -*ness*
- (j) -*th* (as in the noun *depth*, derived from *deep*)
- (k) *in-* (with negative meaning, as in *inedible*)
- (l) *re-* (as in *re-enter*)
- (m) *un-* (as in *unhappy*)

1. Classify these affixes in terms of origin, disinguishing between those borrowed from Latin or French and those inherited from Germanic. (Consult a good dictionary if necessary.)

2. Are the bases to which each affix is attached usually bound or free?

3. How likely is each affix to appear in neologisms, as defined in Chapter 8? For this purpose, assume that the following imaginary words have very recently come into use (perhaps borrowed from a little-known dialect), and are therefore potential bases for the formation of neologisms:

- *bledge* (noun) 'sensation of nausea', as in *Her bledge returned after she had drunk the soup*
- *grint* (verb) 'flatten underfoot', as in *Acorns are easier to grint than horse chestnuts*
- *dorben* (adjective) 'wary, cautious', as in *They are thoroughly experienced and dorben mountaineers.*

If you are not a native speaker of English, ask a friend to judge whether various root-suffix combinations seem plausible, given the word class and meaning of each imaginary word.

4. To what extent do the answers to questions 1, 2 and 3 yield overlapping classifications? Comment on the degree of overlap.

5. What are the Greek-derived technical terms that have the following meanings? Identify the roots (combining forms or free forms) in them, with their meanings. (You may find it helpful to consult a thesaurus, such as Roget's Thesaurus, or an encyclopaedia.)

  (a) 'study of skin diseases'
  (b) 'red blood cell'
  (c) 'flying dinosaur with wing membrane connected to an elongated finger'
  (d) 'situation where political power is in the hands of a small ruling class; members of that class (collectively)'
  (e) 'line on a weather map connecting places with equal temperature'
  (f) 'round submarine vessel for exploring the depths of the ocean'

6. On the basis of the information supplied in this chapter and in Chapter 4, say which of the following distinctions are expressed morphologically in Old English but not modern English, which are expressed in both, and which in neither.

  (a) The distinction between nominative and accusative case in nouns.
  (b) The distinction between third person and other persons (first person 'I' and second person 'you') in the present tense of verbs.
  (c) The distinction between singular and plural in the past tense of verbs.
  (d) The distinction between third person and second person in the plural forms of verbs.

7. Here are pairs of words, each of which shares an Indo-European root. Using a good dictionary, find out for each word in each pair whether the root was inherited via Germanic or was borrowed from some other source.

  (a) *break, fragile*   (d) *dual, two*
  (b) *break, frail*   (e) *nose, nasal*
  (c) *legal, loyal*   (f) *mere* ('lake'), *marine*

Recommendations for reading

On the history of English in general, and on inkhorn terms in particular, see Baugh and Cable (1978). Bauer (1983) has good coverage of what one might call the natural history of word formation, with case studies of particular suffixes such as *-nik*, which enjoyed a considerable vogue in the middle of the twentieth century but has since faded. On more recent developments, see Bauer (1994).

The contemporary morphological consequences of the fact that English vocabulary has two main sources (Germanic and Romance) have been explored extensively within the framework of 'Lexical Phonology' by Kiparsky (1982) and others. For an introduction to this approach, look at Katamba (1993) and then proceed to Kaisse and Shaw (1985). For recent discussion, see Giegerich (1999).

10 Conclusion: words in English and in languages generally

10.1 A puzzle: disentangling lexemes, word forms and lexical items

In this book I have set out to distinguish and elucidate different senses of the word 'word', and to show how they apply in English. The outcome is something of a paradox. Words as basic units of syntactic organisation (the building bricks out of which phrases and sentences are composed) do not coincide exactly with words as items listed in dictionaries. Indeed, there are mismatches in both directions, as we saw in Chapter 2: there are items that need listing but are not words in the grammatical sense, and there are words in the grammatical sense whose meaning and behaviour are so reliably predictable that they do not need listing. There is yet a third sense of 'word', in that items that are words in the grammatical sense (lexemes) may have more than one form, depending on the syntactic context. Yet the items identified by the three criteria resemble each other sufficiently closely so that, in everyday non-technical talk about language, we do not even notice the discrepancies. Why should this be so? Is it so in all languages, or is English peculiar?

These are large questions. On the other hand, given that they arise so naturally out of issues addressed in an introductory text such as this, it is natural to expect that there should be some general consensus among linguistic scholars about how they should be answered. Yet there is no such consensus – something that, as a linguist, I am ashamed to admit. This reflects the meagreness of the research effort that has been devoted to morphology, the lexicon and lexical semantics over the last fifty years, by comparison with the huge intellectual resources devoted to syntax and phonology. So, for want of a consensus and of concerted research, the best that I can offer by way of a reply is speculation – albeit speculation informed by research in inflectional morphology.

10.2 Lexemes and lexical items: possible reasons for their overlap in English

Consider two similar sentences, such as (1) and (2):

(1) Edward sang the solos at the concert.
(2) The solos at the concert were sung by Edward.

Comparing these sentences, we find it natural to try to identify the respects in which they resemble one another and the respects in which they differ. We are likely to say that their lexical content is the same (they exploit the same lexical items), but they differ in that (2) is the passive sentence corresponding to the active sentence at (1). However, we are not inclined to describe (1) and (2) as 'the same sentence', in any sense. The expression 'two forms of the same sentence' has no application for us, whether as ordinary language users or, speaking more technically, as linguists. Probably this is because uttering or understanding a sentence is not usually a matter of recalling a single stored item from the memory – an item with which the sentence can be compared and judged 'the same'. However, for present purposes what matters is simply the fact that (1) and (2) are not 'the same sentence', not the reasons for this fact.

Consider by contrast the following two word forms:

(3) sang
(4) sung

We feel these to be related also, but their relationship is different from that between (1) and (2). There is a clear sense in which, even as non-linguists, we feel them to be 'the same word'. A dictionary will not assign to them two separate entries – or, more precisely, its entries for both *sang* and *sung* will simply refer the reader to the entry for *sing*. In the technical terminology of Chapter 4, *sang* and *sung* are both word forms by means of which, in appropriate contexts, the lexeme SING is expressed. So there is an area of grammar, namely inflectional morphology, where it makes sense to talk of different forms of the same item. Consequently the processes that distinguish the word forms of a lexeme (processes of affix-ation, vowel change or whatever) differ in a fundamental respect from those that distinguish between sentences such as (1) and (2): they relate not different grammatical items but different forms of one item.

As well as being forms of one lexeme, *sang* and *sung* are also forms of one lexical item, for reasons given in Chapter 4: we expect any English verb to have a past tense form and a perfect participle form, so it is not appropriate to record their existence by means of separate dictionary entries for these two forms of every verb. This is so even when their shapes (the word forms that express these grammatical words) need to be recorded because they are irregular; for this irregularity can be noted, where necessary, under a verb's single dictionary entry. But, in the processes that relate these word forms, there is nothing that precludes them from being used to relate forms of distinct lexical items too. The kind of vowel change that relates *sang* to *sing*, and the kind of suffixation that relates *performed* to *perform*, do not come labelled 'not to be used in relating distinct lexical items'. And these morphological processes are indeed used in English for this purpose, as in *song* (a distinct lexical item from *sing*) and *performance* (a distinct item from *perform*).

The existence of phrasal and sentential idioms shows that lexical items can perfectly well be formed by means of syntactic processes, whereby grammatical words are combined. But such word combinations are likely to be longer than the products of morphological processes such as affixation. Moreover, just by virtue of not being words, idioms are likely to less versatile syntactically than words are – that is, to be less convenient to fit into a wide variety of sentence types. So two factors, brevity and versatility, are likely to favour the morphological method over the syntactic method for creating lexical items. That being so, the considerable overlap between lexemes and lexical items becomes more readily understandable, and hence also the tendency to blur the distinction between them by calling them both 'words'.

The account just offered in terms of English presupposes that inflectional morphology has a kind of priority over derivational. The notion 'different word forms belonging to the same word' is peculiar to inflectional morphology, and it is thus in inflectional morphology that processes for relating such word forms play their central role, even though these processes are available for exploitation elsewhere. It is only fair, in an introductory work such as this, to warn that this view of the status of derivational morphology relative to inflectional is not shared by all linguists. But that is not surprising, given what I said in Section 10.1 about the lack of any consensus on reasons for the overlap between 'words' as grammatical items and as lexical items.

10.3 Lexemes and lexical items: the situation outside English

Is the considerable overlap between lexemes and lexical items that is a feature of English found in all languages? This question is really twofold. Firstly, are there languages where the proportion of lexical items that are not lexemes is much higher than in English? We might call these 'idiom-heavy languages', because relatively many of their lexical items would be phrases rather than words. Secondly, are there languages where the proportion of lexemes that are not lexical items is much higher than English? We might call these 'neologism-heavy languages', because relatively many of their words would be items constructed and interpreted 'on-line', like the English sentences at (1) and (2), rather than through identification with remembered items.

A possible example of a language of the first kind is Vietnamese, which has no inflectional morphology and almost no bound morphemes (roots or affixes), and where any distinction between morphological compounds and syntactic phrases is dubious. In Vietnamese, therefore, nearly all polymorphemic lexical items must be analysed as phrasal idioms rather than lexemes (either compound or derived). Among languages that are likely to be more familiar to readers of this book, French too is relatively 'idiom-heavy'. Many concepts that are expressed by compound nouns in English are expressed by phrases in French:

(5) *English*   *French*
    teacup   tasse à thé *(literally 'cup to tea')*
    table wine   vin de table *(literally 'wine of table')*
    sewing machine   machine à coudre *(literally 'machine to sew')*
    hunting permit   permis de chasse *(literally 'permit of hunting')*

It is not that French lacks compounds: for example, *rouge-gorge* 'robin' (literally 'red-throat'), *gratte-ciel* 'skyscraper' (literally 'scrape-sky'), and *essuie-glace* 'windscreen-wiper' (literally 'wipe-screen'). But it is notable that these compounds are all exocentric (a robin is not a kind of throat, and a skyscraper is certainly not a kind of sky). In French, endocentric nominal compounds are relatively scarce by comparison with English; in their place, French makes greater use of phrasal idioms.

Examples of languages of the second kind are the varieties of Inuit, or Eskimo, in which many items whose meaning must be glossed by means of a sentence in English have the characteristics of a morphologically complex lexeme (or a word form belonging to such a lexeme) rather than of a larger syntactic unit. In Eskimo, many more lexemes than in English have the entirely predictable and therefore unlisted character that I ascribed to adverb lexemes such as *dioeciously*. It is as if Eskimo chooses to exploit the morphological route in forming many complex expressions, where many languages would opt for the syntactic route.

Vietnamese and Eskimo represent, if I am right, minimising and maximising tendencies in the grammatical and lexical exploitation of morphology, with English somewhere in the middle. Moreover, most linguists would probably agree that the aspects of Vietnamese and Eskimo that I have emphasised render them rather untypical of human languages in general. Does that mean that, other things being equal, languages exhibit a tendency for lexical items and lexemes to converge? If so, why? Are the factors of brevity and versatility sufficient to explain it? These questions have scarcely been raised in linguistic theory, let alone answered. To pose them in an introductory textbook may seem surprising. I hope that a few readers, encountering them at the outset of university-level language study, may take them as a challenge for serious investigation!

10.4 Lexemes and word forms: the situation outside English

In English, as we have seen, the number of word forms for any given lexeme is small. For verbs, the maximum is five (e.g. *give, gives, gave, giving* and *given* from GIVE) and for nouns the maximum is two (e.g. *performance* and *performances* from PERFORMANCE). That is, English makes relatively little use of inflectional morphology. But, as we have also seen, the picture was quite different a thousand years ago, in Old English. Moreover, Old English is by no means extreme in its use of inflection. In contemporary Turkish, it has been estimated that every verb has about two million forms! This is because a vast array of distinctions that in English are expressed syntactically and by means of pronouns, conjunctions and so on are expressed morphologically in Turkish. For example, the eight-word sentence *We could not get the child to sit* is rendered in Turkish by the two-word sentence *Çocugu oturtamadık*, where *oturtamadık* is analysable as *otur-* 'sit', *-t-* 'cause', *-a-* '(not) be able', *-ma-* 'not', *dı-* 'past', *-k* 'we'.

The behaviour of languages like Turkish demonstrates (if any demonstration is needed) that not every form of every lexeme can be separately memorised. We saw in the previous section that, in Inuit, the great majority of lexemes themselves cannot be separately memorised either, inasmuch as lexemes in Inuit constitute a category as open-ended as sentences are in English. This means that, in a book on Turkish morphology, the equivalent of our Chapter 4 would need to be much more elaborate than here, while in a book on Inuit, the extra elaboration would involve instead (or in addition) Chapters 5 and 6. Consequently, to native speakers of Turkish and Inuit, English morphology may seem rather thin and impoverished. By contrast, to native speakers of Vietnamese, it may seem unnecessarily complicated. So, to the question 'Is English an easy or a difficult language?', no single answer can be given, at least in respect of its morphology. What English does clearly illustrate, however, is the complex mixture of regularity and idiosyncrasy that is characteristic of grammar in general and word structure in particular.

Recommendations for reading

My thinking on the issues tentatively raised in this chapter has been influenced in particular by Di Sciullo and Williams (1987) and Jackendoff (1997). They should not be assumed to agree with anything I say, however.

Systematic comparison of the grammatical characteristics of languages, such as English, Vietnamese and Eskimo, is the domain of linguistic typology. Various introductions to linguistic typology exist, such as Comrie (1989). However, they tend to treat morphology and syntax separately, rather than comparing the relative importance of morphology and syntax in the grammar of different languages, and in particular their relative importance for forming lexical items. Serious work on that issue remains almost entirely in the future.

For information on Vietnamese, a convenient starting-point is Nguyen (1987). A comprehensive description of one variety of Eskimo is Fortescue (1984). The estimate of two million for the number of forms of a Turkish verb is taken from Pinker (1994: 127).

Discussion of the exercises

Chapter 2

1(a) The simple words *break*, *read* and *punish* must clearly be regarded as lexical items, because they do not contain any parts on the basis of which their meaning can be predicted. By contrast, *breaking* and *punishing* have meanings that are clearly predictable on the basis of the meanings of *break* and *punish*, so they need not be listed. *Reading* has this kind of meaning too, as well as on that might be listed, as in *Today's reading is taken from the diary of Anne Frank.*

At first glance, it may seem that *breakable*, *readable* and *punishable* are like the *-ing* set; but the meanings of *readable* and *punishable* are at least partly idiosyncratic, so that a good dictionary would need to list them. A readable book is one whose contents are interesting and entertaining, not one whose text is printed or written legibly. Also, although we talk of punishing a criminal, the adjective *punishable* (as in *punishable with imprisonment*) is usually applied not to people but to the offences that they commit.

The fact that *breakage* and *punishment* have different suffixes, and that these suffixes are not interchangeable (*breakment* and *punishage* are not English words) suggests that these words must be lexically listed. A good dictionary entry for *breakage* will also explain that, although we can break either a plate or a promise, the word *breakage* can be used only for the first, while for the second the word that we use is *breach*.

(b) The words *conceive*, *perceive* and *receive* all contain a common element *-ceive*. However, one cannot identify any clearcut meaning either for this or for the prefixes *con-*, *per-* and *re-* here, so these words must certainly be listed. (The nature of recurring word-pieces such as *-ceive* will be discussed in Chapter 3.)

Receptive and *perceptive* have meanings related to *receive* and *perceive*, but one cannot call their meanings entirely predictable: for example, being receptive to advice involves not just hearing it but acting on it. The absence of a word *'conceptive'*, too, tends to confirm that these words in *-tive* need to be listed.

The words in *-able* look more predictable, but even here we encounter unexpected meanings, as with *readable* at 1(a). *Receivable* appears in modern English mainly in the form *receivables*, with the technical meaning 'debts outstanding, treated as assets by the person to whom the debts are owed'.

The meanings of the abstract nouns in *-tion* are also not entirely predictable, partly because the nouns listed in the question are not the only nouns corresponding to these verbs. Thus, *conceive* has both the meanings 'form in one's mind' and 'become pregnant', yet the noun *concept* corresponds only to the first meaning, unlike *conception*, which corresponds to both. And there is no way of predicting that *reception* has the meaning 'formal social function'.

(c) At first glance, the suffixes *-ness* and *-ly* may seem to be entirely regular in meaning, so that it should not be necessary for a dictionary to list all words containing them. But this is not quite correct. The abstract noun normally corresponding to *high* is not *highness* but *height* (we speak of the height of a building, not its highness); *highness*, by contrast, is virtually restricted to the expression *Her* or *His Royal Highness*. And *highly*, although it may seem close in meaning to *high*, is mainly used with the grammatical function of an intensifier (an alternative to *very*), as in *highly annoying* or *highly likely*. In my variety of English one can readily say *I was highly annoyed* or *A thunderstorm is highly likely*, but *my high annoyance* and *the high likelihood of a thunderstorm* both sound less natural than e.g. *my considerable annoyance* and *the strong likelihood of a thunderstorm*. This sort of divergence between form and meaning will be discussed further in Chapter 8.

4. Examples (a)–(f) all involve the verb *put*. Examples (a) and (b) differ only in the final noun (*hamsters* versus *pigeons*), but this makes a big difference to the lexical items that they contain. Example (b) has an idiomatic meaning ('They caused annoyance by doing something unexpected'), whereas example (a) has only its literal meaning ('They placed a feline among the rodents'). So the phrase *put the cat among the pigeons* is a lexical item (a good dictionary of idioms will certainly list it), but *put the cat among the hamsters* is not.

On the basis of example (c), it seems unnecessary for a dictionary to list the phrase *put out*, because its meaning here ('place outside') is directly derivable from that of its component words *put* and *out*. On the other hand, example (d) would not normally be understood as meaning

'They placed the light outside before going to bed'. Rather, it means 'They extinguished the light ...'. So, with the sense 'extinguish', *put out* counts as a lexical item.

Notice that, whichever sense *put out* has (so whether or not it is a lexical item), the two words *put* and *out* can be separated: *They put the cat out before going to bed* and *They put the light out before going to bed* are perfectly normal alternatives to (c) and (d) respectively. This shows that, even when two words are separated from each other within a sentence, they may still be parts of one lexical item.

Examples (e) and (f) illustrate two semantically contrasting multi-word lexical items: *put oneself out (for someone)* 'go to a lot of trouble (on someone's behalf)' and *put out* 'annoyed'.

Examples (g)–(n) all involve the noun *man*. Of the phrases they contain, the following (with the meanings indicated) are at least in some degree unpredictable and are therefore lexical items:

(h) *a man of his word* 'a man who keeps his promises'
(j) *the man in the street* 'the average person'
(k) *a man about town* 'a fashionable, high-living man'
(n) *best man* 'official supporter of the bridegroom at a wedding ceremony'.

In example (m), *best man* has its literal meaning, so it is not a lexical item; however, example (m) as a whole is a conventional expression, or **cliché**, and so must to that extent be memorised by English speakers, even though its meaning is predictable. This illustrates the fact that knowledge of a language, in its widest sense, involves knowing not only the meanings of lexical items but also social conventions about their use.

Chapter 3

1(a) *tiger-s*, *speak-er-s*. Both words have the English plural suffix *-s*. *Speaker*, meaning 'someone who speaks', can be further divided into *speak* and *-er*; *tiger*, on the other hand, cannot be further divided.

(b) *un-time-ly*, *unique-ly*. Both words contain the suffix *-ly*, whose function I will say more about in Chapter 5. At first sight, the spelling may lead one to think that the two words also contain the same prefix *un-*; however, differences in both meaning and pronunciation show that this cannot be justified.

Because *unique* means '(something) of which there is only one', it may seem sensible to analyse *uni-* here as the morpheme that reappears in e.g. *unicycle* and *unicameral*, meaning 'one'. However, that would leave *-que* as a very unusual cranberry morpheme (a root consisting of less than a syllable); so it seems better to treat *unique* as monomorphemic in modern English, the similarity between *unique* and *uni-* being merely a reflection of their common historical source in Latin.

(c) *decorat-ing, de-centr-al-is-ing*. Both words clearly end with the suffix *-ing*. You may be tempted to split *decorat(e)-* further into *decor* and *-at(e)*, especially as *-at(e)* appears elsewhere in a wide variety of verbs such as *generate, speculate, rotate* and *impersonate*. The question then arises whether the remaining element *decor-* should be treated as the same morpheme as the word *decor*. Similar issues arise in question 5.

It is clear that *decorate* does not contain the negative prefix *de-* that appears in *decentralising*, along with the common suffixes *-al* and *-is(e)* (sometimes spelled *-iz(e)*).

(d) *whole-some, grue-some*. The suffix *-some* is reasonably common in modern English, although brand-new words cannot be formed with it. Other words containing it are *awesome, fearsome, quarrelsome* and *tiresome*. However, the element *grue-* crops up in no other word, so is a cranberry morpheme.

(e) *con-sume-d, con-sump-tion*. The past tense suffix *-(e)d* is clearly identifiable here, as well as the suffix *-tion* that is very common in nouns with abstract meanings (*attraction, perfection, completion* etc.). What is less immediately clear is whether these words should be considered to contain a prefix *con-*, with no consistent meaning. The discussion of example (2) in this chapter suggests that the anwer is yes. Question 2 (discussed below) brings in a further consideration relating to the root.

(f) *erythro-cyte, leuco-cyte*. Any reader who was unfamiliar with these words has probably looked them up and found that they mean 'red blood cell' and 'white blood cell' respectively. This confirms that they are polymorphemic, the morphemes in question being combining forms (derived, in this instance, from Greek).

2. As discussed in the chapter, the plural suffix *-s* on *tigers* and *speakers* has three different allomorphs, [s], [z] and [əz]; in both these examples its shape is [z]. Of the other morphemes identifiable here, *centr(e)-* and *-sum(e)/-sump-* have more than one allomorph. As a word on its own, *centre* has two syllables, but in *decentralising* it has just one; this is connected to the fact that the suffix *-al* that follows it begins with vowel. The *-sump-* allomorph of *-sum(e)* that we find in *consumption* also shows up in *presumption*; it appears before *-tion* and nowhere else. There is a similar parallel between *assume* and *resume* on the one hand and *assumption*

and *resumption* on the other. This constitutes good evidence that all these words really do contain a shared root morpheme, even though it is hard to identify a clearcut meaning for it in contemporary English. Its allomorphs begin with [z] after prefixes beginning with a vowel (*re-*, *pre-*), and with [s] elsewhere; and they end in *-ump-* before *-tion*, *-um(e)* elsewhere. (The existence of an unusual allomorph before *-tion* parallels the allomorphy of *-duce* and *-volve*, discussed in the chapter.)

3. The bound morphemes include the following affixes (affixes being bound by definition): *-s*, *-er*, *un-*, *-ly*, *-ing*, *de-*, *-al*, *-is(e)*, *-some*, *-(e)d*, *con-*, *-tion*. Also bound by definition are Graeco-Latin combining forms, illustrated here by *erythro-*, *leuco-* and *-cyte*. The roots *grue-* and *-sum(e)/-sump-* are also bound, inasmuch as they cannot occur on their own.

With *centre*, the distinction between a morpheme and its allomorphs is important. The morpheme as a whole is clearly free, but its one-syllable allomorph [sentr] (as in *central, centrifugal, centrist*) is bound.

4. Most of the morphemes identified in answer to question 1 have a clearcut meaning, or at least (in the case of the verb-forming suffix *-ate*) a clearcut linguistic function. (See Chapters 4 and 5 for more on the linguistic functions of affixes.) However, this cannot be said of *grue-* or *-sum(e)*. *Grue-* is a cranberry morpheme, occurring only in the word *gruesome*, so it is only *gruesome* as a whole that can be called meaningful, one may argue. As for *-sum(e)*, although it is identifiable as a morpheme in many words (see the discussion of questions 1 and 2), it makes no consistent contribution to their meaning.

5. Three roots in (1b) arguably have free allomorphs: *rend-* in *rendition* (if it is treated as an allomorph of *render*), *clar-* in *clarity* (if it is treated as an allomorph of *clear*), and *applic-* in *applicant* (if it is treated as an allomorph of *apply*).

The existence of words such as *audition, magnificent, clarify* and *applicable* show that their roots are not cranberry morphemes. But the root *leg-* is virtually a cranberry morpheme (as stated in the chapter), and *obfusc-* certainly is, because it occurs nowhere except in *obfuscate*.

If *rend-* in *rendition* is linked to *render*, then it is not a cranberry morpheme, but it could be called a 'cranberry allomorph', since the allomorph *rend-* occurs in no other word.

6. The allomorphy is as follows:

• when the preceding sound is a *t* or *d* sound, as in *wait* or *load*, the [ɪd] allomorph occurs

- otherwise, when the preceding sound is voiceless (as in *rip, lick, watch* or *wash*), the [t] allomorph occurs
- otherwise (i.e. after a vowel or a voiced consonant, as in *drag* or *play*), the [d] allomorph occurs.

The second and third conditions are the same as for the plural -*s*; only the first is different.

Chapter 4

1(a) *Woman* and *women* are forms of the same lexeme, representing the singular of WOMAN and the plural of WOMAN respectively. *Woman's* is not a form of WOMAN because, as explained in the chapter, -*'s* is not an inflectional affix, so *woman's* is formed syntactically rather than morphologically. The adjective WOMANLY and the noun GIRL are different lexemes from WOMAN, although of course related in meaning.

(b) The word form *green* is ambiguous: it can be a form of the adjective GREEN denoting a colour, or of the noun GREEN meaning 'area covered in grass', as in 'village green' or 'bowling green'. In the first sense, *green* is in the same lexeme as the comparative form *greener*; in the second sense, it is in the same lexeme as the plural form *greens* (which is also the sole form of another lexeme GREENS meaning 'vegetables'). In neither sense is *green* in the same lexeme as *greenish*.

(c) *Written* and *wrote* are the perfect participle and the past tense forms of the verb lexeme WRITE. *Writing* may be the progressive form of the same lexeme, or it may be the singular form of the noun WRITING (as in *His writing is illegible*). *Writer* is the singular form of the noun WRITER, and *rewrites* is the third person singular present form of the verb REWRITE, or possibly the plural of the noun REWRITE, with stress on the first syllable rather than the second (as in *Many rewrites were necessary before that novel was accepted for publication*).

2(a) *nooses*; (b) *geese*; (c) usually *moose* (like *sheep, deer*); (d) *played*; (e) *laid*; (f) *lay*; (g) *lied*; (h) *was*; (i) *dived* or, especially in North America, *dove*; (j) *striven* or *strived*; (k) *glided*; (l) *ridden*; (m) see below; (n) *you*; (o) *us*.

To many native speakers, in the context *We have _____ over the hills all day*, none of the forms *strode, stridden* or *strided* sounds quite right. For these speakers, unexpectedly, no perfect participle of STRIDE seems to exist, so the verb is **defective** in this respect.

3(b) *geese*; (f) *lay*; (h) *was*; (i) *dove*; (j) *striven*; (l) *ridden*; (m) *us* are irregular (or, at least, do not follow the majority pattern). Of these, *was* and *us* are suppletive. *Moose* deserves to be called regular, because it follows the special pattern of suffixless plurals for game animals.

The difference in spelling between *played* and *laid* may make it seem that one or the other must be irregular. However, the difference is solely one of spelling; in terms of pronunciation, they are both formed regularly, with the [d] allomorph of the *-ed* suffix. (The form *said* from SAY is not exactly parallel, because it is irregular in pronunciation: [sed].)

4. BAD has the suppletive comparative form *worse* (and superlative *worst*). *Less* may be regarded as a suppletive comparative of LITTLE (e.g. *There is little water in this jug, and there is even less water in that one*). The comparative of FAR, *further* or *farther*, is sufficiently similar to *far* to count as irregular rather than suppletive.

5. The word forms *gentlest*, *commonest* and *remotest* are in general use. (*Remotest* appears in the cliché *I haven't the remotest idea*.) On the other hand, *most precise* sounds better than *precisest*.

Chapter 5

1. The nouns that you are most likely to think of in the first instance are ones denoting the activity of the verb or some result of that activity:

DEFINITION	DEFERENCE, DEFERMENT	DETENTION
REFINEMENT	REFERENCE, REFERRAL	RETENTION
CONFINEMENT	CONFERENCE, CONFERMENT	CONTAINMENT

What is striking here is the lack of consistency among verbs that share the same root. For example, there is no obvious reason why DEFINITION and REFINEMENT should exist while 'DEFINEMENT' and 'REFINITION' do not. To this extent, the existence of DEFINITION and REFINEMENT is unpredictable, and they must be treated as lexical items. The same goes for all these twelve nouns.

Unpredictability of existence does not entail unpredictability of meaning. The meanings of DEFINITION and REFINEMENT are just what one would expect on the basis of the meanings of the corresponding verbs. However, some of these nouns do have more or less unpredictable meanings. CONFINEMENT can have the special meaning 'confinement of a woman in childbirth'. The meanings of CONFERENCE and CONFERMENT are related to distinct non-overlapping senses of CONFER: 'consult or discuss' and 'award or grant' respectively. The same applies to the other nouns with the root *-fer*.

A noun CONTENTION exists, alongside DETENTION and RETENTION, but a moment's thought will confirm that it is derived from CONTEND, not CONTAIN (compare INTEND and INTENTION). There are also nouns CONTINENCE and INCONTINENCE, whose meaning has little now to do with that of CONTAIN but which might still be argued to preserve a derivational relationship to it, in parallel with the relationship between SUSTENANCE and SUSTAIN.

The agentive or instrumental suffix -er can added quite freely to English verbs, and these verbs are no exception; however, of the -er nouns so formed, the only one in common use is CONTAINER, whose meaning is sufficiently idiosyncratic to be lexicalised.

Finally, from REFINE can be formed REFINERY, lexicalised with the meaning 'place where a raw material (e.g. crude oil, sugar cane) is converted into a finished product'.

2. No entirely general method of forming verbs from adjectives exists in English, so any verbs corresponding to these adjectives must be lexical items, even if their meanings are predictable.

The only verb formed solely by prefixation from an adjective in this list is ENRICH. Verbs formed by conversion are EMPTY and HUMBLE. Verbs formed by suffixation are SHORTEN, ACTIVATE and NATIONALISE. Verbs that apparently show prefixation as well as suffixation are REACTIVATE and DENATIONALISE; but these are derived from the verbs ACTIVATE and NATIONALISE rather than directly from ACTIVE and NATIONAL.

There are no verbs derived from FULL, POOR, LONG and PROUD. That is not to say that English has no words to express the corresponding meanings (e.g. 'cause to be full' or 'become full'): in fact, there are verbs FILL, IMPOVERISH and LENGTHEN. FILL is arguably derived from FULL, but if so the process involved is an idiosyncratic vowel change, unparallelled elsewhere. The relationship between LONG and LENGTHEN parallels that between STRONG and STRENGTHEN, discussed in the chapter.

The lack of a verb corresponding to PROUD seems at first sight strange, given the existence of a verb (HUMBLE) corresponding to an adjective that means the opposite of PROUD. But this seems less strange when one notices that PROUD denotes only a mental state, while HUMBLE can relate also to external circumstances, independent of mental state; and the verb HUMBLE (like HUMILIATE) relates primarily to external circumstances. (A person who is humbled in defeat does not necessarily acquire humility!)

Of the verbs we have noted, some are transitive only (IMPOVERISH, ENRICH, NATIONALISE and HUMBLE); ones that may also be intransitive are FILL, EMPTY, LENGTHEN, SHORTEN, and perhaps ACTIVATE.

3. The suffix -ism is often attached to proper names, to mean 'doctrine

associated with X': e.g. BUDDHISM, MARXISM, THATCHERISM. It also crops up with other noun bases (e.g. TOURISM, CONSERVATIONISM, ALCOHOLISM), and with some bases whose word class is hard to determine because they are bound (e.g. ASTIGMATISM, NEPOTISM, DYNAMISM, PESSIMISM).

4. The suffix -ful, attached to nouns, can have the meaning 'amount that can be contained in X', e.g. MOUTHFUL, HANDFUL, SPOONFUL, BOXFUL.

5. Adjectives derived by means of -ly are not numerous, but some of them are common: e.g. FRIENDLY, COSTLY, BEASTLY, MANLY, GHOSTLY (from nouns), and KINDLY, GOODLY, CLEANLY (from adjectives). This adjectival -ly is not combinable with the adverb-forming -ly, however. Some English speakers, including me, find acceptable the adverb SILLILY formed from SILLY, where the first -ly is not a suffix but part of the root, but reject the adverb *FRIENDLILY formed from the already suffixed adjective FRIENDLY. Notice that the word form kindly can represent either the adverb KINDLY 'in a kind fashion' or the adjective KINDLY 'kind-hearted'. Similarly, chiefly can represent either an adjective formed from the noun CHIEF (as in his chiefly authority) or an adverb from the adjective CHIEF (as in They chiefly eat rice alongside Their chief food is rice).

6. Your list of -ar adjectives probably includes examples such as POLAR, SOLAR, LUNAR, REGULAR, NUCLEAR, CIRCULAR, MODULAR, LINEAR and CELLULAR. In all of these, the base contains the sound /l/. By contrast, most adjectives in -al have bases that lack /l/ (although there are some exceptions, e.g. LOCAL, FLORAL).

7. The technique is to construct verbal and nominal contexts where cook can appear, and then see what other verb-noun pairs can appear in the same or similar contexts. Consider:

(i)   They cooked all the food.
(ii) The cooks were busy.

For cooked in (i), one can substitute baked, sold or organised, and in (ii) one can substitute bakers, sellers or organisers. Since these agent nouns are derived from the corresponding verbs by suffixation of -er, it seems reasonable to treat the noun COOK as derived from the verb COOK too, although without a suffix. (The suffixed noun COOKER also exists, but denotes an appliance rather than a person.)

8. Let us first try using DOG as the core, or base, for affixation. Actual or possible words include DOGGIE 'little dog', DOGGY 'dog-related',

UNDOGGISH 'not dog-like'; less likely but still possible as a jocular creation IS DE-DOGGIFICATION 'removal of dogs (and things related to dogs) from' (-ific- being the allomorph of -ify that appears before -ation, as in MAGNIFICATION, derived from MAGNIFY). However, even DE-DOGGIFICATION uses only three affixes. One can do more with COMPARTMENT. With two prefixes and three suffixes, one can form REDECOMPARTMENTALISATION, with the meaning 'the process of again reversing distribution into compartments'. This is a lexeme that you have almost certainly never met, but it is a conceivable (though inelegant) item of technical jargon.

Chapter 6

1(a) *Moonlight* is a NN compound noun (and hence a lexeme), with the expected stress on the first element. *Moonscape* is too, but it is unusual in that *-scape* is a bound morpheme, found also in *landscape* and *seascape*. *Harvest moon* has an institutionalised meaning (the full moon closest to the end of September in the northern hemisphere), but is nevertheless a phrase rather than a compound. The same goes for *blue moon*, which is a phrase inside a phrasal idiom (see Chapter 2).

(b) *Blueberry, bluebottle* and *greybeard* are AN compound nouns. *Sky-blue* is a NA compound adjective. *Blue-pencil*, meaning 'censor' or 'cut', is a verb derived by conversion from a nominal source (see Chapter 5), but the source is not a word but rather a phrase (*blue pencil* as a conventional term for what a censor uses in crossing out objectionable passages). It is therefore a phrasal word rather than a compound.

(c) *Pencil case, eyebrow pencil* and *pencil sharpener* are NN compound nouns; *eyebrow pencil* also contains the NN compound noun *eyebrow*. *Pencil-thin* is a NA compound adjective. *Thin air* is not a word but a phrase (though it is part of a cliché).

(d) *Airport* and *air conditioning* are NN compound nouns. (The stress on *air* rather than on *conditioning* supports the analysis as a compound rather than a phrase.) *Air force* is also a NN compound noun, but *Royal Air Force* is a phrase consisting of an adjective and a noun, just like *effective air force* or *royal palace*; the fact that *the Royal Air Force* is lexicalised as a name for the British air force does not affect its status as a phrase. *Air France* presents the same analytic dilemma as *governor general* does: is it a lexicalised phrase in which the modifier (*France*) follows the head (*Air*), or is it a left-headed compound noun? Either way, the pattern is unusual, though not without parallels in proper names of companies or institutions (e.g. *Air Canada, Virgin Atlantic, Tate Modern*). Perhaps this structure is popular in such names because, being head-first, it has a whiff of sophistication derived from the head-first structure of noun phrases in French (where nouns generally precede adjectives).

(e) *Silkworm* and *T-shirt* are NN compound nouns. *Silk shirt*, however, is a phrase consisting of a head noun (*shirt*) and a modifier (*silk*) which also happens to be a noun.

(f) The plural of *lady-in-waiting* is *ladies-in-waiting*, not *lady-in-waitings, which shows that, like *brother-in-law*, it is a noun phrase, not a word (despite the hyphens). All the other examples are nouns, pluralised by adding *-s* at the end, but their structure is that of a phrase (e.g. *stick in the mud, want to be*) rather than a word, so they are not compounds but phrasal words.

(g) *Overrún* is a compound verb of PV shape, from which the noun *óver-run* is formed by conversion (see Chapter 5), with a stress shift – the same stress shift as seen in (for example) the nouns *tórment* and *prótest*, formed from the verbs *tormént* and *protést*. *Undercoat* is a compound noun of PN shape, from which the verb *undercoat* is formed by conversion, but here there is no stress shift. (Compare other denominal verbs such as *father* in *to father a child* and *commission* in *to commission a portrait*; these also show no change in the stress pattern of the base noun.) *Underhand* is an adjective consisting of a preposition and a noun, so, although *under hand* is not a well-formed phrase, it makes sense to analyse it in the same way as *offshore* and *in-house*, discussed in Section 5 of the chapter. *Hándover* is a noun derived by conversion from a verbal source, but this source is a phrase rather than a word (*hand over*, as in *they handed the money over*); it thus resembles *blue-pencil* in (b) above, except that the conversion is in the opposite direction.

2(a) *Moonlight* and *moonscape* are both endocentric.

(b) *Blueberry* and *sky-blue* are endocentric. *Bluebottle* is also endocentric, because, although a bluebottle (whether a kind of fly, a kind of plant or a kind of jelly-fish) is not a bottle, its name likens it metaphorically to one. On the other hand, *greybeard* is exocentric because it denotes not a kind of beard nor something that resembles a beard, but rather someone who typically has a grey beard (an old man). *Blue-pencil* is also exocentric because, though a verb, it has no verbal head.

(c), (d), (e) All are endocentric.

(f) None of these is a compound, so the question does not apply.

(g) *Overrún* (verb) and *undercoat* (noun) are endocentric. Their derivatives by conversion, *óverrun* and *undercoat* (verb), are exocentric, as are *underhand* (an adjective with no adjectival head) and *handover* (a noun with no nominal head).

3. The only secondary compounds are *pencil sharpener* and *air conditioner*, in which *pencil* and *air* are interpreted as objects of the verbal elements *sharpen* and *condition* (the latter being a verb derived by conversion from a noun).

4. *breakfast* plus *lunch*; *motor* plus *hotel*; *radio detecting and ranging*; *modulator* plus *demodulator*; *light amplification by stimulated emission of radiation*.

5. *nano-* 'one thousand millionth (or billionth) of'; also in *nanometer*
    proto- 'first'; also in *protozoon*
    -plasm 'predominant substance in living cells'; also in *cytoplasm*
    endo- 'internal'; also in *endogamy*
    -centric 'having a centre'; also in *polycentric*
    poly- 'many'; also in *polycentric*
    -phony 'sound'; also in *telephony*
    leuco- 'white'; also (with different spelling) in *leukaemia*
    -cyte 'cell'; also in *cytoplasm* and *erythrocyte*
    omni- 'all'; also in *omniscient*
    vorous 'eating'; also in *carnivorous*
    octa- 'eight'; also in *octagon*
    -hedron 'surface'; also in *polyhedron*

Chapter 7

1. In these tree diagrams, an italicised item is the head of the smallest constituent that contains it, e.g. the suffix *-y* (or *-i-*) is the head of *greedy*, and *-ness* is the head of *greediness*.

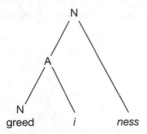

(The change from *-y* to *-i-* in *greediness* is purely orthographic, with no linguistic significance.)

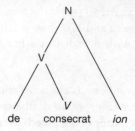

Arguably, *consecrate* is itself complex, with a verb-forming suffix *-ate* added to a base *consecr-*, in turn consisting of a prefix *con-* and a bound root *secr-*, perhaps an allomorph of *sacred*. However, no clearcut meaning can be assigned to *con-*. (Problems in analysing this kind of word were discussed in Chapter 2.)

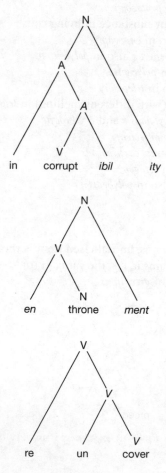

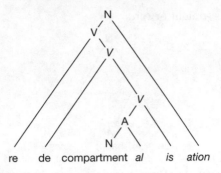

The compounds are all right-headed, like this one:

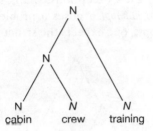

All the other compounds illustrated are contained within the largest compound, so only the structure of this largest one needs to be given:

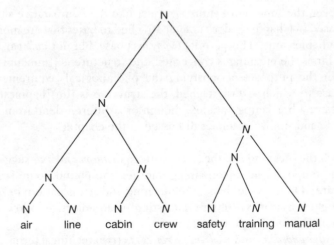

According to the revised generalisation about stress formulated in Section 7.4, the main stress in this compound should be on *safety* – which seems correct.

2. *Unhappiness* is straightforward:

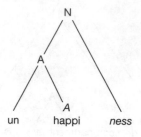

The alternative structure [un-[[happi-ᴀ]-ness]ₙ]ₙ is implausible because *un-* does not normally attach to nouns: **unjoy*, **ungrief*, **unfolly*, **uncompassion*. There are only a few exceptions: *unease, unrest, unconcern*.

On the other hand, *unhappiest* poses a problem. On the basis of its meaning, 'most unhappy', one expects the structure to be:

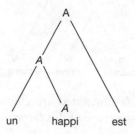

However, the superlative suffix *-est* (just like the comparative suffix *-er* discussed in Chapter 5) does not get attached to bases that are more than two syllables long. This permits *happy* as a base, but not *unhappy*. It is as if, so far as the meaning is concerned, the structure is [[unhappi-]-est], but for the purposes of satisfying the phonological requirements for the base to which *-est* is attached, the structure is [un-[happiest]]. We thus have a bracketing paradox, though of a different kind from *nuclear physicist* and similar examples discussed in the chapter.

3. Both the meaning and the stress pattern of *íncome tax rate* suggest that it is a compound noun containing another compound noun: [[income tax] rate]. On the other hand, the meaning and stress pattern of *high táx rate* suggest that it is a phrase consisting of an adjective followed by a compound noun: [high [tax rate]].

In *value ádded tax* and *goods and sérvices tax* (two technical terms used in different countries for the same kind of tax), the immediate components seem clearly to be *value added, goods and services*, and *tax*. But is the whole item a phrase or a compound word? The fact that *value added* and *goods and services* are themselves phrases rather than words suggests the former; however, the fact that the stress is on the first component (rather than on *tax*) suggests that these are compounds of the kind that contain lexicalised (or at least institutionalised) phrases. (Compare the phrase *inefficient services*, which is not lexicalised: it sounds odd to say '*inefficient sérvices tax*' with the meaning 'tax on inefficient services'.)

It was suggested that *French history teacher* might have the meaning 'teacher of French history' even when bracketed [French [history teacher]]. But no comparable bracketing for *goods and services tax* seems plausible, because it contains the conjunction *and*. This reinforces the counterargument based in the chapter on the implausibility of the bracketing [fresh [air fiend]].

Chapter 8

1. In my own active vocabulary, the forms that exist are indicated with ticks:

	-ment	-al	-ence	*stress shift*
confer	✓		✓	
defer	✓		✓	
infer			✓	
prefer	✓		✓	
refer		✓	✓	
transfer			✓	✓

What this shows is that, although various noun-forming processes can be used with verbs in *-fer*, only *-ence* can be used with all of them. It is thus these forms (*deference, inference* etc.) that are formally the most regular. But that does not mean that *-ence* is semantically regular. For example, there is no way of predicting from the meaning of *confer* that *conference* corresponds semantically only to the meaning 'discuss' rather than to the meaning 'grant, award' (for which the corresponding noun is *conferment*). This confirms that, in word formation, formal regularity does not entail semantic regularity.

2. The corresponding past tense forms are *bound, blinded, found, minded, reminded* and *wound*. (This last form is spelled the same as *wound* 'injure', but is of course pronounced differently.) At first sight, it looks as if, even among these verbs, *-ed* suffixation is the regular way of forming the past, with just three exceptions that use vowel change instead. But *blind* 'make sightless' and *mind* 'pay attention to', as verbs, are arguably derived by conversion from an adjective and a noun respectively, while *remind* is

derived from *mind*. Only *bind*, *find* and *wind* are basically verbs – and these are precisely the verbs within this group that use vowel change. So there is a case for saying that vowel change, not *-ed* suffixation, is the regular way of forming the past tense for basic verbs in *-ind* – that is, that the *-ed* form is blocked by the *-ound* form, which conforms to a smaller-scale formal regularity affecting only three verbs.

3. (a) (i) *singer*
       (ii) 'someone who sings'

   (b) (i) *cook* (formed by conversion from the verb)
       (ii) 'appliance for cooking'

   (c) (i) *thief*
       (ii) The word *stealer* is not often used on its own, but occurs in metaphorical contexts, such as *scene-stealer* 'actor who attracts the attention of the audience to himself or herself, at the expense of other actors'.

   (d) (i) *cyclist*
       (ii) The word *cycler* is not used except in contexts specifying a destination or location, such as *She is a regular cycler to work* meaning 'She regularly cycles to work'.

   (e) (i) *spy*
       (ii) It is hard to think of any context where '*spier*' might naturally occur.

   (f) (i) *cleaner* (with the sense 'clean buildings, e.g. offices, as an occupation')
       (ii) The word *cleaner* can also mean a substance used in cleaning, as in *oven-cleaner*.

   (g) (i) There is no word that means 'someone who habitually prays'.
       (ii) The word *prayer* exists, but is normally pronounced as one syllable rather than two, in which case it has the meaning 'activity of praying' or 'utterance used in praying' rather than 'person who prays'.

   (h) (i) *flautist, flutist* or *flute-player*
       (ii) *flute-player* means 'someone who plays the flute'.

The suffix *-er* is the most general and regular of the agent suffixes (meaning 'someone who Xs'). However, for words of the form *Xer*, the agent meaning is blocked if some other word exists with that meaning, as in (b), (c), (d) and (e). The term *flautist* at (h) might be expected to block *flute-*

player or *flutist*, but *flautist* is rather technical and not in wide common use, so the three terms exist side by side.

The divergence between formal and semantic regularity is illustrated by *cooker* and *cleaner*. Both are regularly formed, but are more or less irregular semantically in that *cooker* never means 'someone who cooks' and *cleaner* does not always mean 'someone who cleans'.

4. With adjectival bases, the suffix *-ish* creates adjectives with the consistent meaning 'somewhat X'. It is therefore semantically regular. The fact that some such derivatives are often listed in dictionaries (e.g. *greenish*, *whitish*) while others are not (e.g. *longish*, *slowish*) tends to suggest that these adjectives lack formal regularity. However, in my speech (though not in writing) almost any adjective can be a suitable base, as in *fastish*, *toughish*, *boringish*, *importantish*. For me, therefore, when suffixed to adjectives, *-ish* is both semantically and formally regular.

With noun bases, *-ish* usually means 'resembling X' (e.g. *boyish*, *babyish*) or 'appropriate for X' (e.g. *slavish*, *bookish*, *tigerish*), often with a derogatory connotation, but it can also mean 'of nationality or group X' (e.g. *Swedish*, *Amish*), with no such connotation. It is therefore not entirely regular semantically. Formally, too, it is irregular in that some of its bases are bound allomorphs (e.g. *English*, *Irish*, *Spanish*), others free (e.g. *Scottish*, *Finnish*); also in that some nouns that one might expect to serve as bases for *-ish* suffixation do not. e.g. *snakish*, *armyish*, *Chinish*, *Greecish*. What is more, these examples sound (to my ear) less plausible, or more contrived, than e.g. *aggressivity* and *languidity*, discussed in the chapter. Suffixation of *-ish* to nouns, unlike suffixation of *-ity* to adjectives, thus displays no evident formal regularity. With respect to both kinds of regularity, therefore, *-ish* words formed from adjectives differ from ones formed from nouns.

Chapter 9

1. Germanic: *-ful*, *-ing*, *-less*, adverb-forming *-ly*, adjective-forming *-ly*, *-ness*, *-th*, *un-*.
Latin or French: *-able*, *-ity*, *-ive*, *in-*, *re-*.

2(a) *-able*: Mostly attaches to free bases (indeed, it can attach to almost any semantically appropriate transitive verb, e.g. *wipable*, *understandable*, *pleasable*), but sometimes also to bound ones (e.g. *formidable*, *palpable*, *potable*).

(b) *-ful*: Almost always attaches to free bases (a rare bound base being *aw-* in *awful*, which, because of meaning change, can no longer be plausibly regarded as an allomorph of *awe*).

(c) *-ing*: Attaches only to free bases.

(d) *-ity*: Attaches to some free bases (e.g. *density, maturity*), but more often to bound ones. Some of these bound bases are morphemes with no free allomorphs (e.g. in *paucity, garrulity*). Others are bound allomorphs of morphemes that are free in some contexts (e.g. *sanity*, whose base, rhyming with *pan*, has also a free allomorph *sane* that rhymes with *pane*; and *sensitivity*, whose base is stressed *sénsitive* when free).

(e) *-ive*: Like *-ity*, attaches to more bound bases (e.g. *sensitive, aggressive, receptive, compulsive*) than free ones (e.g. *defensive, disruptive*).

(f) *-less*: Like *-ful*, attaches mostly to free bases, although some of its bases have lost their freedom historically (e.g. *ruthless* 'without compassion').

(g) *-ly* (as in the adverb *happily*): Always attaches to free bases.

(h) *-ly* (as in the adjective *manly*): Almost always attaches to free bases (a rare bound base being *come-* in *comely* 'attractive').

(i) *-ness*: Always attaches to free bases.

(j) *-th*: Attaches to some free bases (*warm-th, tru-th*), but more often to a bound allomorph of an otherwise free base, as in *leng-th, streng-th, wid-th, bread-th*.

(k) *in-*: Attaches mostly to free bases, as in *in-sane, in-tangible*, also to some bases that are so rare in a positive context (without negative *in-*) that they have effectively become bound, e.g. *in-exorable, in-defatigable*. The same applies to its allomorph [ɪ], spelled *in-, im-, il-* or *ir-*, and alluded to in Section 5.6.

(l) *re-*: As noted in Chapter 3, we need to distinguish between *re-* as it is pronounced in *re-store* 'store again' and *re-* as it is pronounced in *restore* 'repair'. The latter often appears with bound bases, e.g. in *recede, retain, refer*. However, the *re-* of *re-enter* is the former, which is limited to free bases.

(m) *un-*: Almost always attaches to free bases (rare bound bases being *-couth, -kempt* and *-ruly* in *uncouth, unkempt* and *unruly*).

3. To my ear, the neologisms *grintable, bledgeful, dorbening, bledgeless, dorbenly, dorbenness, regrint, undorben* sound more plausible words than *dorbenity, bledgive, bledgely, dorbenth, indorben*. I would not expect a native

speaker to disagree with me over more than one or two of these items. My classification is therefore:

- likely in neologisms: *-able*, *-ful*, *-ing*, *-less*, adverb-forming *-ly*, *-ness*, *re-*, *un-*
- unlikely in neologisms: *-ity*, *-ive*, adjective-forming *-ly*, *-th*, *in-*.

4. Putting together the results of from questions 1–3, we arrive at the following table:

	Source	Status of bases	In neologisms
-able	not Germanic	mostly free	yes
-ful	Germanic	almost all free	yes
-ing	Germanic	all free	yes
-ity	not Germanic	mostly bound	no
-ive	not Germanic	mostly bound	no
-less	Germanic	almost all free	yes
adverbial *-ly*	Germanic	all free	yes
adjectival *-ly*	Germanic	almost all free	no
-ness	Germanic	all free	yes
-th	Germanic	mostly bound	no
in-	not Germanic	mostly free	no
re-	not Germanic	all free	yes
un-	Germanic	almost all free	yes

This confirms the suggestion in the chapter that, if an affix is Germanic, it is likely to attach to free bases, and to be available for neologisms. The correlation is not exact, however, since *-th* and adjective-forming *-ly* are exceptions. Conversely, if an affix is borrowed from Latin or French, we will expect it to attach mainly to bound bases and to be unavailable for neologisms, although *in-* and *-able* are each an exception to one of these expectations, and *re-* is an exception to both.

5. (a) *dermatology. -derm(at)-* 'skin', *-(o)logy* 'science, area of expertise'
   (b) *erythrocyte. erythr(o)-* 'red', *-cyt(e)-* 'cell'
   (c) *pterodactyl. -pter(o)-* 'wing', *-dactyl-* 'finger'
   (d) *oligarchy. olig(o)-* 'few', *-archy* 'rule'
   (e) *isotherm. is(o)-* 'equal', *-therm(o)-* 'heat'
   (f) *bathy-* 'deep', *sphere*

Of these, all are bound combining forms except *sphere*. *Therm* occurs as a free form; but, as such, it means not 'heat' in general but 'unit of heat equivalent to 100,000 British Thermal Units', so should probably be regarded as a distinct morpheme from the combining unit *-therm(o)-*.

6(a) In Old English, this distinction was expressed morphologically in some nouns, but not in all. In modern English, it is expressed in personal pronouns (*I/me*, *she/her*, *he/him* etc.), but not in nouns.

(b) This distinction is expressed in both Old and Modern English (Modern English *(I/you) help* versus *(he/she) helps*; Old English *(ic) helpe*, *(ðū) helpest*, *(hē/hēo) helpeð*). Notice, however, that Old English, unlike Modern English, also distinguishes first person from second person.

(c) This distinction is expressed in Old English but not in Modern English. In the past tense, Old English distinguishes number (singular versus plural) but not person, while Modern English makes no morphological distinctions at all (except in *was/were*).

(d) This distinction is expressed neither in Old nor in Modern English. Even in Old English, all the plural forms are alike in any one tense (present or past) or mood (indicative or subjunctive). Any readers who know German will be able to confirm that, in this respect, Old English differs from German, where second person plural forms can be distinguished from third person plural ones (e.g. *(ihr) kommt* 'you (plural) come' versus *(sie) kommen* 'they come').

7. (a) *break* inherited; *fragile* borrowed from Latin
   (b) *break* inherited; *frail* borrowed from French
   (c) *legal* borrowed from Latin; *loyal* borrowed from French
   (d) *dual* borrowed from Latin; *two* inherited
   (e) *nose* inherited; *nasal* borrowed from Latin
   (f) *mere* inherited; *marine* borrowed from Latin

Glossary

accusative case – grammatical **case** usually exhibited by a noun phrase functioning as the direct object of the verb, and usually (but by no means always) expressing semantically the goal or patient of the action that the verb denotes.

acronym – blend incorporating only the initial letters of its components, e.g. *NATO* for *North Atlantic Treaty Organisation*. (Abbreviations such as *USA* or *BBC*, in which the name of each letter is pronounced in turn, are not acronyms.)

adjective – see **word class**.

affix – **prefix** or **suffix**.

affixation – process of adding an affix.

allomorph – one of the variant pronunciations of a morpheme, among which the choice is determined by context (phonological, grammatical or lexical). For example, [z], [ɪz] and [s] are phonologically determined allomorphs of the plural suffix, occurring respectively in *cats*, *dogs* and *horses*. A morpheme with only one pronunciation is sometimes said to have only one allomorph.

allomorphy – choice of allomorphs, or (in respect of a morpheme) the characteristic of having more than one allomorph.

argument – noun phrase or prepositional phrase that is a required or expected concomitant of a verb. For example, *sleep* normally has one argument (*The boy slept*) while *kick* has two (*The boy kicked the ball*) and *introduce* has three (*The boy introduced his sister to the visitors*).

article – see **word class**.

bahuvrihi – another term for **exocentric**, drawn from the terminology of traditional Sanskrit grammarians.

base – word or part of a word viewed as an input to a derivational or inflectional process, in particular affixation.

binary – of a tree diagram, having two branches (or no more than two branches) at each node.

blend – kind of compound in which at least one of the components is reproduced only partially, e.g. *smog*, combining elements of *smoke* and *fog*.

blocking – see **semantic blocking**.

bound morpheme, bound allomorph – morpheme or allomorph that cannot stand on its own as a word. A bound morpheme is one whose allomorphs are all bound. See also **free morpheme**.

bracketing – see **labelled bracketing**.

bracketing paradox – inconsistency between the structure suggested by the syntactic or morphological properties of an expression and the structure suggested by its meaning.

case – grammatical category expressing the relationship of a noun phrase to the verb in its clause. See also **nominative, accusative**.

causative verb – verb meaning 'cause to (be) X'. For example, the verb *boil* is causative in the sentence *Ellen boiled the water*, meaning 'Ellen caused the water to boil'.

circumfix – a two-part affix, one part preceding and the other following the base.

cliché – expression that resembles an **idiom** in that it is conventional or institutionalised, but differs from an idiom in that its meaning is entirely derivable from the meanings of its components.

cognate – of words, derived from the same historical source. For example, the English word *father* and the French word *père* are cognate, both being descended (through Proto-Germanic and Latin respectively) from the same Proto-Indo-European word.

collocational restriction – restriction whereby a word, in the context of (or when collocated with) another specific lexeme, has a literal meaning different from its usual one. For example, the meaning 'not sweet' for the adjective *dry* is restricted to the collocation *dry wine*.

combining form – bound morpheme, more root-like than affix-like, usually of Greek or Latin origin, that occurs only in compounds, usually with other combining forms. Examples are *poly-* and *-gamy* in *polygamy*.

comparison – grammatical category associated with adjectives. Many English adjectives distinguish basic, 'comparative' and 'superlative' forms (e.g. *hot, hotter, hottest*).

compound – word containing more than one root (or combining form). See also **primary compound, secondary compound**.

conjunction – see **word class**.

conversion – the derivation of one lexeme from another (e.g. the verb FATHER from the noun FATHER) without any overt change in shape. Some linguists analyse this phenomenon as **zero-derivation**.

cranberry morph(eme) – morpheme (or allomorph) that occurs in only one word (more precisely, only one lexeme).

defective – term applied to a lexeme that lacks one or more of the grammatical words (and the associated word forms) that most lexemes of its class possess. For example, the archaic verb lexeme QUOTH 'said' (as in *quoth he*) is defective in that it has only a past tense form.

derivational morphology – area of morphology concerned with the way in which lexemes are related to one another (or in which one lexeme is derived from another) through processes such as affixation. For example, the verb lexeme PERFORM is derivationally related to the nouns PERFORMANCE and PERFORMER.

determiner – see **word class**.

duality of patterning – parallel divisibility of speech into both meaningless units (sounds, syllables) and units with meaning or grammatical function (morphemes, words).

endocentric (of a compound or derived word) – possessing a head. See also **exocentric**.

exocentric (of a compound or derived word) – lacking a head. For example, the noun *sell-out* is exocentric because it contains no component that determines its word class (*sell* being a verb and *out* being an adverb).

formal generality – of a derivational process, the characteristic of being **formally regular** and also of exploiting all or nearly all potential bases, without idiosyncratic 'gaps'. The formation of verbs with the suffix *-en*, although formally regular, is not entirely general because it exhibits gaps: for example, there are no verbs '*wetten*', '*blunten*' or '*limpen*' corresponding to the adjectives *wet, blunt* and *limp*.

formal regularity – of a derivational process, the characteristic that the kind of base to which the process can apply can be relatively precisely specified. For example, the formation of verbs with the suffix *-en* is formally regular in that nearly all its bases are monosyllabic adjectives ending in obstruents (plosives and fricatives), e.g. *tough, fat, damp*.

free morpheme, free allomorph – morpheme or allomorph that can stand on its own as a word. A morpheme may have both free and bound allomorphs, e.g. *wife* is free but *wive-* is bound because it appears only in the plural word form *wives*.

gender – syntactically and morphologically relevant classification of nouns, present in Old English (as in modern German and French) but lost in modern English. The gender to which an animate noun belongs may be determined by sex (hence the use of terms such as 'feminine' and 'masculine' for individual genders), but for most inanimate nouns in Old English gender was semantically arbitrary.

grammatical word – the lexemic and grammatical content of a word form in a given context. For example, in the context *She rows the boat*, the word form *rows* represents the grammatical word 'third person singular, present tense, of the verb ROW', while in the context *two rows of beans* the same word form represents the grammatical word 'plural of the noun ROW'.

hapax legomenon – in classical studies, a word that is 'said only once', i.e. a lexeme of which only one token occurs in the entire corpus of Greek literature (or Roman literature, in the case of Latin words).

head – element within a compound or derived word that determines the syntactic status, or word class, of the whole word. Semantically, also, a compound noun whose head is X usually denotes a type of X. For example, *house* is the head of the compound *greenhouse*. Many linguists would also analyse some derivational affixes as heads, e.g. *-er* as the head of the noun *teacher*.

idiom – expression whose meaning is not predictable on the basis of the meanings of its components.

inflectional morphology – area of morphology concerned with changes in word shape (e.g. through affixation) that are determined by, or potentially affect, the grammatical context in which a word appears. See also **lexeme**.

intransitive verb – verb that is not **transitive**.

irregular (of inflected word forms) – formed differently from the corresponding word form for the majority of lexemes in the word class. Most linguists regard irregularity as a matter of degree; thus for example, *went* as the past tense form of GO is more irregular than *bent* (instead of **bended*) as the past tense of BEND, both because *bent* is not suppletive and because there are other past tense forms that follow the same pattern, e.g. *lent, sent* from LEND, SEND. See also **formal regularity, semantic regularity**.

labelled bracketing – an alternative to a **tree diagram** as a way of representing the internal structure of words. See Chapter 7.

lexeme – word seen as an abstract grammatical entity, represented concretely by one or more different inflected word forms according to the grammatical context. Where the distinction is important, lexemes are conventionally represented in small capitals while word forms are in italics. For example, the verb lexeme PERFORM has four inflected word forms: *perform, performs, performing* and *performed*.

lexical category – see **word class**.

lexical item – linguistic item whose meaning is unpredictable and which therefore needs to be listed in the **lexicon** or in dictionaries.

lexical semantics – the study of the meaning relationships between lexical items, and how these relationships are structured.

lexicon – inventory of lexical items, seen as part of a native speaker's knowledge of his or her language.

monomorphemic – consisting of only one morpheme.

morpheme – minimal unit of grammatical structure. (The morpheme is often defined as the minimal *meaningful* unit of language; but that definition leads to problems, as explained in Section 3.5.)

morphology – area of grammar concerned with the structure of words and with relationships between words that involve the morphemes that compose them.

neologism – newly coined word.

node – see **tree diagram**.

nominal – belonging to the word class 'noun', or having the characteristics of a **noun**.

nominative case – grammatical **case** exhibited by a noun phrase functioning as the subject of the verb, and usually (but by no means always) expressing semantically the agent of the action that the verb denotes.

noun – see **word class**.

number – grammatical category associated especially with nouns. In English, 'plural' and 'singular' numbers are distinguished inflectionally (e.g. *cats* versus *cat*).

object – see **transitive verb**.

onomatopoeia – resemblance between the sound of a word and what it denotes, e.g. in *cock-a-doodle-do*.

open class – word class to which new members can be added, i.e. noun, verb, adjective or adverb, but not preposition, pronoun, determiner or conjunction.

part of speech – see **word class**.

periphrastic form – phrase that expresses a grammatical word when no appropriate word form exists, e.g. *more interesting* for 'comparative of INTERESTING'.

person – grammatical category associated especially with pronouns, identifying individuals in relation to the speaker and hearer. English distinguishes 'first person' (*I, we*), 'second person' (*you*) and 'third person' (*he, she, it, they*).

phonology – area of grammar concerned with how speech sounds function to distinguish words in a language (and in languages generally). The scope of phonology includes how sounds are related, how they are combined to form syllables and larger units, and how relationships between syllables are indicated by features such as stress.

phrasal word – item that has the structure of a phrase but functions syntactically like a word.

polymorphemic – consisting of more than one morpheme.

prefix – bound morpheme that precedes the root.

preposition – see **word class**.

primary compound (or **root compound**) – compound in which neither component functions semantically as an argument of a verbal element in the other component. The commonest primary compounds in English are of the noun–noun type, e.g. *doorknob, lamp post, mosquito net*.

pronoun – see **word class**.

regular – complying with a rule; (of inflected word forms) formed in the same way as the corresponding word form for the majority of lexemes in the word class. See also **formal regularity, semantic regularity**.

right-headed – having its rightmost element as its **head**.

root – within a non-compound word, the morpheme that makes the most precise and concrete contribution to the word's meaning, and is either the sole morpheme or else the only one that is not a prefix or a suffix. In English, especially in its inherited Germanic vocabulary, most roots are free. For example, the roots of *unhelpfulness, cat* and *vision* are respectively *help, cat* and *vis-* (which recurs in *visible*). See also **stem, base**.

root compound – see **primary compound**.

secondary compound (or **verbal** or **synthetic compound**) – compound in which one component functions semantically as an argument of a verbal element in the other component. In the commonest secondary compounds in English, the verbal element is in the second component, e.g. *sign-writer, paint-remover, window cleaning*.

semantic blocking – the phenomenon whereby the existence of a word (whether simple or derived) with a particular meaning inhibits the morphological derivation, even by formally regular means, of another word with precisely that meaning.

semantic regularity – of a derivational process, the characteristic of making a uniform and consistent contribution to the meanings of the lexemes produced by it.

semantics – the study of meaning, especially as part of the wider study of how knowledge of language is organised. See also **lexical semantics**.

sound symbolism – within a group of words, partial similarity in sound correlated with a similarity in meaning, as in *slip, slurp, slide, sleek, slither*.

stem – term used in various senses: **root**, or **base** in general, or base for the word forms of a lexeme (involving the addition of inflectional affixes only, not derivational ones).

subject – within a sentence, the noun phrase with which the verb may agree in person and number (in English), as in *The boy wakes up* (with suffix *-s*) versus *The boys wake up*. The subject often, but not always, denotes the agent or instigator of the action denoted by the verb.

suffix – bound morpheme that follows the root.

suppletion – phenomenon whereby one lexeme is represented by two or more different roots, depending on the context; for example, the verb GO is represented by *wen(t)* in the past tense and *go* elsewhere.

syncretism – phenomenon whereby, in systematic fashion, two grammatical words associated with the same lexeme are represented by the same word form. For example, regular verbs in English (those with *-ed* in the past tense) syncretise the past tense form (e.g. in *Mary organised the concert*) and the perfect participle form (e.g. in *Mary has organised the concert*).

synthetic compound – see **secondary compound**.

tense – grammatical category exhibited by verbs, closely associated with time. In English, a distinction between present and past tenses is expressed inflectionally, e.g. in *give* and *wait* versus *gave* and *waited*.

token – instance or individual occurrence of a **type**. For example, the sentence *Next week I go to Edinburgh and next month Alice arrives from Washington* contains two tokens of the word form *next*. Equivalently, the word form *next*, as a type, is instantiated twice in this sentence.

transitive verb – verb that is accompanied (generally or in a particular context) by a noun phrase fulfilling the syntactic function of 'object', denoting usually the goal or patient of the action of the verb. For example, in *John eats before going to work*, both *eats* and *going* are intransitive, but, in *John eats breakfast before going to work*, *eats* is transitive, its object being *breakfast*.

tree diagram – a way of representing the structure of a complex word or sentence in terms of a branching structure in which the branching points (**nodes**) and the ends of the branches may bear word class or phrasal labels. For examples, see Chapter 7.

type – see **token**.

verb – see **word class**.

verbal compound – see **secondary compound**.

word – fundamental unit out of which phrases and sentences are composed. See also **grammatical word, lexeme, lexical item, word form**.

word class – one of the classes to which words (more precisely, lexemes) are allocated on the basis of their grammatical behaviour, including **noun** (e.g. *cat, disappointment*), **verb** (e.g. *perform, come*), **adjective** (e.g. *green, sensitive*), adverb (e.g. *happily, well*), **preposition** (e.g. *on, without*), **pronoun** (e.g. *she, us*), **determiner** (e.g. *this, our, the*), **article** (e.g. *a, an, the*), **conjunction** (e.g. *and, if, because*).

word form – word viewed as a pronounceable entity, representing concretely a lexeme in some grammatical context. One word form may be shared by more than one lexeme; for example, [rouz] is shared by the noun ROW 'line of objects' (as its plural form), the noun ROSE (as its basic, or singular, form), the verb ROW 'propel with oars' (as its third person singular present tense form), and the verb RISE (as its past tense form).

zero-derivation – the derivation of one lexeme from another by means of a phonologically empty, or 'zero', affix. See also **conversion**.

References

Adams, Valerie (1973), *An Introduction to Modern English Word-Formation*, London: Longman.

Anderson, Stephen R. (1992), *A-Morphous Morphology*, Cambridge: Cambridge University Press.

Aronoff, Mark (1976), *Word Formation in Generative Grammar*, Cambridge, MA: MIT Press.

Aronoff, Mark (1994), *Morphology by Itself: Stems and Inflectional Classes*, Cambridge, MA: MIT Press.

Baayen, Harald (1992), 'Quantitative aspects of morphological productivity', in Geert Booij and Jaap van Marle (eds), *Yearbook of Morphology 1991*, Dordrecht: Kluwer, pp. 109–49.

Bauer, Laurie (1983), *English Word-Formation*, Cambridge: Cambridge University Press.

Bauer, Laurie (1988), *Introducing Linguistic Morphology*, Edinburgh: Edinburgh University Press.

Bauer, Lauric (1994), *Watching English Change*, London: Longman.

Bauer, Laurie (1998), 'When is a sequence of two nouns a compound in English?', *English Language and Linguistics*, 2: 65–86.

Baugh, Albert C. and Thomas Cable (1978), *A History of the English Language*, 3rd edn, London: Routledge & Kegan Paul.

Carstairs-McCarthy, Andrew (1992), *Current Morphology*, London: Routledge.

Carstairs-McCarthy, Andrew (1993), 'Morphology without word-internal constituents: a review of Stephen R. Anderson's *A-Morphous Morphology*', in Geert Booij and Jaap van Marle (eds), *Yearbook of Morphology 1992*, Dordrecht: Kluwer, pp. 209–33.

Clark, Eve V. (1993), *The Lexicon in Acquisition*, Cambridge: Cambridge University Press.

Comrie, Bernard (1989), *Language Universals and Linguistic Typology: Syntax and Morphology*, 2nd edn, Oxford: Blackwell.

Corbin, Danielle (1987), *Morphologie dérivationnelle et structuration du lexique* (2 vols), Tübingen: Niemeyer.

Di Sciullo, Anna Maria and Edwin Williams (1987), *On the Definition of Word*, Cambridge, MA: MIT Press.

Fortescue, Michael (1984), *West Greenlandic*, London: Croom Helm.

Giegerich, Heinz J. (1999), *Lexical Strata in English: Morphological Causes, Phonological Effects*, Cambridge: Cambridge University Press.

Gil, David (2000), 'Syntactic categories, cross-linguistic variation and universal grammar', in Petra M. Vogel and Bernard Comrie (eds), *Approaches to the Typology of Word Classes*, Berlin: Mouton de Gruyter, pp. 173–216.

Hinton, Leanne, Johanna Nichols and John J. Ohala (eds) (1994), *Sound Symbolism*, Cambridge: Cambridge University Press.

Hogg, Richard and C. B. McCully (1987), *Metrical Phonology: A Coursebook*, Cambridge: Cambridge University Press.

Jackendoff, Ray (1975), 'Morphological and semantic regularities in the lexicon', *Language*, 51: 639–71.

Jackendoff, Ray (1997), *The Architecture of the Language Faculty*, Cambridge, MA: MIT Press.

Jakobson, Roman and Linda Waugh (1979), *The Sound Shape of Language*, Brighton: Harvester Press.

Jelinek, Eloise and Richard A. Demers (1994), 'Predicates and pronominal arguments in Straits Salish', *Language*, 70: 697–736.

Kaisse, Ellen and Patricia Shaw (1985), 'On the theory of lexical phonology', *Phonology Yearbook*, 2: 1–30.

Katamba, Francis (1993), *Morphology*, Basingstoke: Macmillan.

Kiparsky, Paul (1982), 'From cyclic phonology to lexical phonology', in Harry van der Hulst and Norval Smith (eds), *The Structure of Phonological Representations (Part I)*, Dordrecht: Foris, pp. 131–75.

Liberman, Mark and Alan Prince (1977), 'On stress and linguistic rhythm', *Linguistic Inquiry*, 8: 249–336.

Lieber, Rochelle (1983), 'Argument linking and compounds in English', *Linguistic Inquiry*, 14. 251–85.

Lieber, Rochelle (1992), *Deconstructing Morphology: Word Formation in Syntactic Theory*, Chicago: University of Chicago Press.

Marchand, Hans (1969), *The Categories and Types of Present-Day English Word-Formation*, 2nd edn, Munich: C. H. Beck.

Matthews, P. H. (1991), *Morphology*, 2nd edn, Cambridge: Cambridge University Press.

Nguyen, Dinh-Hoa (1987), 'Vietnamese', in Bernard Comrie (ed.), *The World's Major Languages*, London: Croom Helm, pp. 777–96.

Pinker, Steven (1994), *The Language Instinct: How the Mind Creates Language*, New York: William Morrow.

Pinker, Steven (1999), *Words and Rules: The Ingredients of Language*, New York: Perseus Books.

Selkirk, Elisabeth O. (1982), *On the Syntax of Words*, Cambridge, MA: MIT Press.

Spencer, Andrew (1988), 'Bracketing paradoxes and the English lexicon', *Language*, 64: 63–82.

Spencer, Andrew (1991), *Morphological Theory*, Oxford: Blackwell.

Index

Note: This index covers only Chapters 1–10, not the glossary. Many terms listed in the index are also defined in the glossary.